T0323600

Cambridge Elements ≡

Elements in the Philosophy of Immanuel Kant
edited by
Desmond Hogan
Princeton University
Howard Williams
University of Cardiff
Allen Wood
Indiana University

KANT ON THE HISTORY AND DEVELOPMENT OF PRACTICAL REASON

Olga Lenczewska
Florida State University

CAMBRIDGE
UNIVERSITY PRESS

Shaftesbury Road, Cambridge CB2 8EA, United Kingdom

One Liberty Plaza, 20th Floor, New York, NY 10006, USA

477 Williamstown Road, Port Melbourne, VIC 3207, Australia

314–321, 3rd Floor, Plot 3, Splendor Forum, Jasola District Centre,
New Delhi – 110025, India

103 Penang Road, #05–06/07, Visioncrest Commercial, Singapore 238467

Cambridge University Press is part of Cambridge University Press & Assessment,
a department of the University of Cambridge.

We share the University's mission to contribute to society through the pursuit of
education, learning and research at the highest international levels of excellence.

www.cambridge.org
Information on this title: www.cambridge.org/9781009565141

DOI: 10.1017/9781009216760

First published 2025

A catalogue record for this publication is available from the British Library

ISBN 978-1-009-56514-1 Hardback
ISBN 978-1-009-21678-4 Paperback
ISSN 2397-9461 (online)
ISSN 2514-3824 (print)

Kant on the History and Development
of Practical Reason

Elements in the Philosophy of Immanuel Kant

DOI: 10.1017/9781009216760
First published online: January 2025

Olga Lenczewska
Florida State University

Author for correspondence: Olga Lenczewska, olenczewska@fsu.edu

Abstract: This Element's focus is Kant's history of human reason: his teleological vision of the past development of our rational capacities from their very emergence until Kant's own "age of Enlightenment." One of the goals is to connect Kant's speculative account of the very beginning of rationality – a topic that has thus far been largely neglected in Kantian scholarship – to his well-known theory of humankind's progress. The Element elucidates Kant's hopes with regard to reason's future progress and his guidelines for how to achieve this progress by unifying them with his vision of reason's past. Another goal is to bring more attention to Kant's essay "Conjectural Beginning of Human History," where this account is presented, and to show that this unusual text does not stand in conflict with Kant's philosophy and is not merely tangentially related to it, but illuminates and complements certain aspects of his critical philosophy.

Keywords: Kant, Enlightenment, conjectural history, reason, maturation

ISBNs: 9781009565141 (HB), 9781009216784 (PB), 9781009216760 (OC)
ISSNs: 2397-9461 (online), 2514-3824 (print)

Contents

Introduction

For Kant, the history of human reason is a history of our species' gradual emancipation from nature and, subsequently, from unjust political arrangements.[*] Far from being a merely empirical description of various past events, as some commentators have mistakenly suggested,[1] history involves teleological reflection and constitutes a part of Kant's critical philosophy. History is created when reason looks back on the seemingly chaotic sequence of human affairs and imposes reflective judgment on it,[2] unraveling in this way a unified, teleological pattern of humankind's progress, which amounts to reason's past development and self-determination. The ability to create history is unique to our species because it requires both existing within nature (a characteristic we share with other animals) and possessing the faculty of reason (of which other animals are devoid).[3] Therefore, as Allison specifies, "the main reason why humankind for Kant has a history" is that "the complete development of the predispositions that involve the use of reason will require an indeterminately lengthy historical process, because reason cannot develop fully within the lifetime of any individuals, but only gradually in the species as a whole."[4]

The focus of this Element is Kant's history of human reason: his teleological vision of the past development of our rational capacities from their very emergence until Kant's own "age of Enlightenment."[5] One of the goals of this Element is to connect Kant's speculative account of the very beginning of rationality[6] – a topic that has thus far been under-explored and under-studied in Kantian scholarship – to his well-known theory of humankind's progress. By

---

[*] In this Element I will be using the following abbreviations for the titles of Kant's works: Anth-Fried – *Anthropology Friedländer*, Anth-Mron – *Anthropology Mrongovious*, Anth-Mensch – *Anthropology Menschenkunde*, Anth-Busolt – *Anthropology Busolt*, IUH – "Idea for a Universal History with a Cosmopolitan End," WIE – "What is Enlightenment?," CB – "Conjectural Beginning of Human History," WOT – "What Does It Mean to Orient Oneself in Thinking?," G – *Groundwork for the Metaphysics of Morals*, CPrR – *Critique of Practical Reason*, CJ – *Critique of the Power of Judgment*, MM – *Metaphysics of Morals*, TP – "On the Common Saying," Rel – *Religion within the Boundaries of Mere Reason*, TPP – *Perpetual Peace*, Anth – *Anthropology from a Pragmatic Point of View*, Ped – *Lectures on Pedagogy*, L-Log – *Lectures on Logic*.

[1] White Beck, for instance, writes: "Philosophy, for Kant, is a priori knowledge from concepts; history is empirical, not a priori, knowledge of human events" (White Beck 1963, xviii).

[2] See, for example, IUH, 8: 17, CJ, 5: 425–34, Anth-Busolt, 25: 1436. When it comes to the difference between determinative and reflective judgment, "[t]he difference turns on the question of whether the rule, which includes concepts, laws, and principles, is given or whether what is given is merely some particular content that is to be subsumed under a sought-for rule. In the former case, the function of judgment is determinative; in the latter it is reflective" (Allison 2009, 29).

[3] Kant's conception of reason will be elaborated on in what follows.   [4] Allison 2009, 27.

[5] WIE, 8: 40.

[6] This account is presented in "Conjectural Beginning" and in Kant's lectures on anthropology from various years.

doing so, I hope to elucidate Kant's hopes with regard to reason's future progress and his guidelines for how to achieve this progress by unifying them with his vision of reason's past. Another goal of this Element is to bring more attention to Kant's essay "Conjectural Beginning of Human History" (1786), where a large part of this account is presented, and to show that this, as Yovel puts it, "somewhat unusual"[7] text does not stand in conflict with Kant's critical philosophy and is not merely tangentially related to it, but actually illuminates and complements certain aspects of Kant's critical philosophy.

This Element is divided into three sections. Section 1 introduces Kant's speculations about the transition our species underwent from nonrational animals into primitive, rational humans. It also shows how these speculations fit with Kant's broader view of the development of humans' reason, or of the species' gradual process of learning how to make a mature, enlightened use of reason.

Section 2 focuses on a text in which the speculative account of the beginning of human history is presented in most detail: "Conjectural Beginning of Human History." I defend the exegetical importance of this essay for Kant's practical philosophy by arguing that the claims Kant makes in it are not merely fictional or imaginative, but play a key role in his teleological view of the progression of human history. I also assess the contribution that Kant makes to the conjectural history genre through this essay and discuss how distinct it is from the most prominent and well-studied conjectural histories of the Enlightenment era.

Section 3 focuses on what Kant's account of the history of reason tells us about his political and pedagogical guidelines for the continuance of humanity's progress toward the fulfillment of its vocation and for the progress of any given individual. I also present and defend my understanding of what it means to think and act in an enlightened (or as Kant also calls it, a "pluralistic") way, connecting this idea to the three maxims of good thinking, the public use of reason, and the role of interpersonal communication in advancing our rational capacities.

1 The Emergence and Trajectory of Reason

1.1 Introduction

Kant's teleological account of humankind's rational progress, which Kant himself divided into three phases – cultivation, civilization, and moralization[8] – has been widely studied in connection with his historical, anthropological,

---

[7] Yovel 1989, 190.

[8] Kant mentions these phases in IUH, 8: 26, Anth, 7: 324, Ped, 9: 449–50, and several other places. Humans, for example, are the only species capable of choosing its own interests and purposes, the only species that can change its nature through intergenerationally transmitted knowledge, and the only one that seeks to realize its vocation.

pedagogical, and religious writings. The differences between us and other animals are typically a point of departure from which Kant's view of human history is analyzed. But Kant's critics rarely discuss his views about the way in which humankind's rational progress might have *begun* and the circumstances surrounding this beginning. Implicit in such an omission is the assumption that Kant does not say much about the very beginning of human history or that whatever he does say is of little philosophical value.

In this section of the Element, I seek to challenge these assumptions. To do so, I begin by looking at Kant's various conjectural and more literal remarks about the transition our species underwent from mere irrational animals into primitive humans possessing a rudimentary form of rationality (Section 1.2). Once I have reconstructed Kant's account of the pre-history of reason, I proceed to show how it fits with his broader view of humankind's rational progress and its subsequent stages (Section 1.3).

1.2 The "Discovery" and First Use of Reason

Kant does offer an account of the circumstances in which humankind's rational progress began. It is presented in most detail in "Conjectural Beginning of Human History," but it can also be found in the notes from his lectures on anthropology (1772–89), in the published *Anthropology from a Pragmatic Point of View* (1798), and in the *Lectures on Pedagogy* (1802). To connect this account within a broader context of Kant's view on human history, we need to look at an even broader array of his works, such as "An Answer to the Question: What is Enlightenment?" (1784), "Idea for a Universal History with a Cosmopolitan Aim" (1784), *Critique of the Power of Judgment* (1790), *Religion within the Boundaries of Mere Reason* (1793), and *Perpetual Peace* (1795).

It is likely to be questioned how serious Kant's account of humankind's beginning presented in "Conjectural Beginning" is – especially in light of his own admission that the story presented in this essay has been written by "venturing on a mere pleasure trip."[9] However, a more careful reconstruction of this story and a better grasp on the epistemic status of the seemingly historical claims presented in it will show that it fits very well with Kant's understanding of human history (and, consequently, that it should be regarded with a similar degree of seriousness): as a post facto reflection that imposes a priori conditions for our comprehension of certain phenomena in order to help us make these phenomena intelligible, while *not* making claims as to their ontological status or empirical accuracy.

My reconstruction of Kant's account of humankind's beginning in this section will proceed as follows. I will start in Section 1.2.1 by presenting his

---

[9] CB, 8: 109.

speculative anthropological description of the soon-to-be-human animals in the state of nature and their lives *before* the beginning of human history, relying on several texts mentioned. While doing so, I will draw attention, on the one hand, to the ways in which the soon-to-be humans resembled other animals and, on the other hand, to the ways in which they were unique even before becoming humans proper. Next, in Section 1.2.2 and Section 1.2.3 I will discuss Kant's account of our *transition* from mere animals to human beings, which marks the very beginning of rationality and human history, in "Conjectural Beginning." I will also provide a framework for a proper understanding of this essay and the literary tradition in which it was written. Finally, drawing on Kant's anthropological writings and transcriptions of his anthropology lectures, in Section 1.2.4 I will discuss the ways in which the newly emerged human being after the awakening of reason differs from other animals.

1.2.1 Human Animals in the State of Nature

Several versions of the notes from Kant's anthropology lectures include a section about the character of the human species, where we can find his speculations about the kind of animal the human being is qua a part of nature. This question is an appropriate question to ask, Kant ensures us, since "in the system of nature, the human being belongs to the animal kingdom."[10] At times, this question is approached from a historical perspective and focuses not only on the animalistic aspects of our nature, but also on our supposed prehistorical existence in the state of nature, when we would have been merely animals.[11] Given the similarities in these speculations across the notes from Kant's anthropology lectures from different years, and given that these remarks are repeated in the published version of these lectures (1798), it is reasonable to believe that the views expressed in these notes are reliably Kant's.

Kant draws on the scientific (biological, geographical, and archeological) findings available to him and claims that it is likely that the human being as an animal would have been determined by nature to walk on four feet, he would have been carnivorous, and he would have achieved sexual maturity and general independence around the age of thirteen.[12] Next, Kant frequently considers the question whether the human being as animal would have been a predator or not, and admits that we do not have enough evidence to speculate about this, or – in the notes from later years and the published *Anthropology* – that he would have likely been a predator.[13]

---

[10] Anth-Mron, 25: 1415.   [11] Anth-Mensch, 25: 1197.

[12] AP 25:246, Anth-Fried, 25: 675–76, Anth-Mron, 25: 1415–16, Anth-Mensch, 25: 1194–95, Anth, 7: 322–23.

[13] Anth-Mron, 25: 1416, Anth, 7: 322.

But Kant's speculations about the prehistorical animal that would soon become a human being do not only concern its physical characteristics. In the Mrongovious transcription of his lectures (1784–85) Kant also mentions the possibility that the prehistorical 'human' would have not had to work due to only having needs and desires that can be easily satisfied by nature itself – something that shows a very significant influence of Rousseau's second *Discourse* on him. Kant writes: "The crude state of nature was good in some respects, since human beings inclined toward noble simplicity and did not know any needs or desires (though only out of ignorance) ... [H]uman beings nourished themselves from trees like apes and did not need to work due to a lack of needs."[14] Next, in his lectures Kant frequently turns to the question whether the prehistorical 'human' would have been social or solitary. He admits that neither alternative seems quite right, at which point it becomes clear that the human being is a *unique* type of animal.[15]

The Mrongovious transcription of Kant's anthropology lectures dates from about the same time as "Conjectural Beginning of Human History" (1786). In the latter, Kant similarly speculates about the nature of prehistorical 'humans' before they became humans proper. These prehistorical 'humans,' who belonged only to the animal kingdom, would not have had free will or the capacity to act rationally. They would have been fully guided – causally determined – by their natural instincts with regard to both actions and desires.[16] More specifically, they would have been guided by a strong sense of smell and its affinity with taste, and therefore they would have instinctively known what food is suitable and unsuitable for them.[17] Additionally (as in the Mrongovious lecture notes), Kant speculates here that the prehistorical 'human' would have been satisfied with his existence ("As long as the inexperienced human being obeyed this call of nature, he did well for himself") and would have not been worried about his future.[18] Importantly, he would have also perceived himself as equal to others of his kind and equal to other species of animals.

Perhaps the most intriguing question when considering Kant's speculative account of our animal nature before we became humans proper is: what allowed *our* species in particular (as opposed to other species) to make it possible for us to become rational animals? Kant speculatively provides several characteristics that might have allowed for such a transition – upright posture, walking on two feet, the position of our digits, and complex vocal communication.[19] However, he does not explain how these characteristics might have come about, but only

---

[14] Anth-Mron, 25: 1418.   [15] Anth-Mron, 25: 1416.   [16] CB, 8: 111.   [17] CB, 8: 111.
[18] CB, 8: 111.   [19] CB, 8: 110–11, Anth-Mensch, 25: 1196–97, Anth, 7: 323.

speculates that they had to come about in order for this transition to take place. These features would have allowed us to learn several primitive technical skills that we could not do instinctually (such as swimming) and to teach these skills to our offspring.[20]

1.2.2 A Conjectural History of Reason's Awakening

Interestingly, while Kant speculates about our prerational nature in a number of texts, he only speculates about the actual *transition* that our species made from mere animals to humans proper (to rational animals) in one place: in the "Conjectural Beginning" essay. According to Yovel, the central theme of this text is "not the history of reason proper but what may be called its pre-history; for it does not discuss the progress of reason toward maturation, but goes back to explore the more primordial and obscure stage, at which human reason had first broken away from 'the womb of nature' and established itself as an independent principle, higher than nature and opposing it."[21] Chakrabarty, similarly, states that what is "at the heart of this essay" is "[t]he opposition between the animal life of the human species and its moral life."[22] Before reconstructing this account, however, I want to set the stage for a proper understanding of this highly unusual text by providing a brief characterization of conjectural histories (something I will return to in more detail in Section 2).

"Conjectural Beginning" is written within the Enlightenment literary tradition of "conjectural histories" – a term coined by the first theorist of this genre, Dugald Stewart, in the early nineteenth century. This genre was very popular between 1750 and 1800, and all of the major Enlightenment thinkers from Prussia, France, and Scotland – such as Hume, Rousseau, Herder, Smith, and Ferguson – wrote at least one, and often more, conjectural histories.[23] The aim of conjectural histories was to provide a speculative account of the prehistoric origins of human society and of the origins and developments of various cultural phenomena: language, the arts, social norms, or legal practices. Inspired by new reports from travelers to societies hitherto unfamiliar to Europeans, the Enlightenment thinkers attempted to work out the stages that humankind must have gone through in order to form the first societies and to gradually shape them into ones with recognizable political, religious, and economic institutions. This genre assumes that there is a series of identifiable transitional steps between primitive human existence and fully fledged society, and that human

---

[20] CB, 8: 111, Anth, 7: 322–23, Ped, 9: 445.   [21] Yovel 1989, 191.

[22] Chakrabarty 2016, 384.

[23] The most famous one, of course, is Rousseau's *Discourse on the Origin and Foundations of Inequality among Men*.

nature is universal (thus yielding itself to such theorization).[24] For instance, Adam Smith's *Lectures on Jurisprudence* (1750s–1760s), which Dugald Stewart (the first theorist of conjectural histories who coined the term to define this genre) recognizes as a prototypical conjectural history, present a four-stage history of social life: hunting, herding, farming, and commence. Each of these stages is characterized by its own distinct institutions and modes of subsistence, developed based on the distinct needs of people living during a given stage.

As I have said before, while Kant presents his teleological view of human history in a number of texts, he only speculates about its very beginning – about the actual *transition* that our species made from mere animals to humans proper – in one place, and he chooses to frame these speculations as a conjectural history. In "Conjectural Beginning," Kant wants to neither reconstruct the distant past in detail (which, as he explicitly admits, would be empirically impossible given the limitations of our knowledge of the history of primitive human beings), nor, on the other hand, provide us with an entirely imagined and implausible story (which he would regard as useless for his anthropological and ethical purposes).[25] Rather, he wants to sketch a way in which our species' rational capacities might have emerged and initially progressed – a way of presenting past events for which a conjectural history is perfectly suitable.

By sketching such an account, Kant wants to complement his teleological view of the progression of human history. His purpose in this text is not to claim that our rational capacities could have only emerged under the exact historical conditions sketched in this essay. Rather, the story presented in it is a possible way in which they might have emerged that, regardless of whether it is historically accurate, sheds light on the nature of these capacities. This method of acquiring and presenting knowledge about the world resembles the way in which the sciences are sometimes practiced. Specifically, Kant's conjectural story resembles the kind of scientific explanatory models called "minimal models,"[26] which present "a story about why a class of systems will all display the same large-scale behavior because the details that distinguish them are irrelevant" and are used to "explain patterns of macroscopic behavior across systems that are heterogeneous at smaller scales."[27]

Since the "Conjectural Beginning" essay is mostly of use for Kant's *practical* philosophy and since it is a conjectural exercise, it might be reasonable to put aside the question whether the story presented in it really took place in the far past, and view it instead as merely possible from the theoretical perspective,

---

[24] Smalligan Marušić 2017.   [25] CB, 8: 109. See also IUH, 8: 29.
[26] Batterman & Rice 2014.   [27] Batterman & Rice 2014, 349.

while useful from the practical perspective. In other words, we are permitted, from the practical philosophical standpoint, to think of our rational capacities as having emerged in a way described in this essay.

1.2.3 The Beginning of Human History

Having set the stage for understanding this essay and the epistemic status of claims made in it, I now want to reconstruct the account of our exit from the state of nature presented in it. Kant's starting point when sketching the beginning of human history in "Conjectural Beginning" are creatures that are in a position to become rational beings. In other words, they live not in a completely crude state of nature, but in a position to exit it. These individuals are physically prepared for this transition by virtue of being able to stand and walk upright, communicate about abstractions, and teach themselves several primitive technical skills.[28] Loosely (sometimes even ironically) drawing on the biblical book of Genesis,[29] Kant also posits that these individuals are a heterosexual couple who do not live in physical proximity to other individuals of their kind, and who live in a temperate climate abounding in opportunities for nourishment and secured against predators.[30] By virtue of belonging only to the realm of nature, this couple is fully "guided" or determined by "[natural] instinct, that *voice of God* which all animals obey."[31]

Once Kant has characterized the two individuals in a position to exit the state of nature, he proceeds to sketch a speculative account of their first use of reason (which, we will soon see, marks their exit from the state of nature). At some point in time, Kant writes, one of the soon-to-be humans recognized within himself the ability to notice other possibilities for acting than the ones given by instinct, and thus the ability to invent desires independently of his natural instinct. (Unfortunately, Kant provides no explanation why this happened exactly when it did or why it happened at all. But he posits the appropriate natural [physical, geographical] circumstances for this realization to take place.) Kant writes: "*reason* soon began to stir and sought through comparison of that which gratified with that which was represented to him by another sense than

---

[28] CB, 8: 110–11.

[29] "Conjectural Beginning" may be viewed as Kant's response to Herder's own account of the early stages of humankind, which itself largely draws on the biblical Genesis. Unlike Kant's essay, Herder's *Oldest Document of Humankind* (1774) takes the Bible to be a literal, historically reliable account of humanity's beginning. Herder writes: "No one will doubt that the first Mosaic chapters are *documents, Origines*; for they contain reports of the most ancient matters of humankind" (Herder 1774/2015, 90). Kant criticizes Herder's treatment of Genesis by being explicit in "Conjectural Beginning" that a historiography based on the Bible is only of conjectural and speculative value (Wood 2007, 160–62; Beiser 1987, 149–52).

[30] CB, 8: 110.   [31] CB, 8: 111.

the one to which instinct was bound, such as the sense of sight, as similar to what previously was gratifying, to extend his knowledge of the means of nourishment beyond the limits of instinct."[32] This ability to compare options for acting, the creation of new desires that go beyond nature (and even against it), and the ability to *choose* how to act in order to satisfy a particular desire was the first manifestation of the human faculty of reason and reason's first step of elevating the human being above other animal species. Zimmer's interpretation of this moment supports mine:

> Kant reads the eating of the forbidden fruit not as the mere giving in to temptation, but as that which for the first time indicates the possibility of choice. It is precisely this newfound ability to choose one's own way of life which marks the human – now fully human – from the animal. The discovery of choice is what Kant calls the first step of reason to become fully realized.[33]

The success of the first attempt to act independently from nature made the human, as Kant puts it, "conscious of [his] reason as a faculty that can extend itself beyond the limits within which all animals are held."[34] The human noticed his reason's purposive capacity to determine his ends – to act rationally, according to practical maxims chosen by himself. He "discovered within himself a faculty of choosing for himself a way of living and not of being bound to a single one, as other animals are."[35] This "first attempt at a free choice" marked the beginning of our species' emancipation from the animal kingdom and the tutelage of nature into the "estate of freedom."[36] By having resisted the instinctive impulse (synonymous in this essay with the voice of God) to eat from the tree of life, the human being emancipated himself from the tutelage of nature.[37]

Kant's speculative account of the first use of reason in "Conjectural Beginning" differs in style and form from his well-known critical works, but it can nonetheless be articulated in terms familiar from his critical philosophy. Doing so might help us see the conceptual connections between the ideas presented in this essay and those presented in his other works.

When Kant describes the first human's becoming conscious of his reason as a faculty that can extend itself beyond natural instincts, this awareness can be understood as awareness of his capacity to act in accordance with the technical hypothetical imperative and in accordance with the pragmatic hypothetical

---

[32] CB, 8: 111. [33] Zimmer 2022, 185. [34] CB, 8: 111–12. [35] CB, 8: 112.

[36] CB, 8: 112.

[37] This theme echoes also in Kant's *Lectures on Pedagogy*, where he notes that while animals are not capable of choosing a plan for their life and are limited by their natural instinct, the human being differs from them in not having an instinct and being capable of using their mental powers in a variety of ways (LP, 9: 441).

imperative. Technical hypothetical imperatives are those grounded on any contingent end (means-end reasoning), whereas pragmatic hypothetical impera-tives are grounded on achieving the assertoric end of happiness (prudential reasoning).[38] Both of these abilities are exercised when the first human chooses to eat a piece of fruit against the guidance of his natural instincts. Kant's depiction of the soon-to-be human in the condition of animality before the first use of reason makes it clear that such an individual lacked the capacity for prudential reasoning or reasoning by virtue of pragmatic hypothetical impera-tives. This is the crucial capacity that is discovered, as it were, through and in the first use of reason. This discovery of the ability to invent desires independ-ently of one's natural instinct can be therefore understood as the discovery of the ability to reason prudentially.

It is less clear, however, whether the soon-to-be human in the condition of animality before the first use of reason also lacked the less advanced capacity for technical hypothetical imperatives (means-end reasoning), since Kant mentions that he had a degree of technical skill. Things get even more complicated if we look at what Kant says about the skills of the animals who were to become humans in his *Anthropology*. There, in the section "The Character of the Species," Kant states clearly that human beings are distinguished from other animals by three predispositions: the technical predisposition for manipulating things, the pragmatic (prudential) predisposition for using others for their own purposes, and the moral predisposition.[39] Given that he includes the first predisposition in the list of things that make us different from other animals, it would seem that this predisposition or capacity is unique to humans proper. But a more plausible interpretation, I believe, is that the animals who were to become humans were already different from other animal species even before they become humans proper by exercising reason. This idea makes sense in light of Kant's characterization of the unique physical features of the soon-to-be humans, such as walking on two feet. So even if the soon-to-be human was able to act somewhat in accordance with the technical hypothetical imperative before the first use of reason, this does not mean that this ability was available to other animal species as well[40] – in fact, it is not even clear from Kant's writings whether the technical predisposition can manifest itself in the absence of the pragmatic predisposition.

Kant's speculative account of the first use of reason in "Conjectural Beginning" can also be articulated in terms of the familiar triad of the stages

---

[38] G, 4: 414–17.   [39] Anth, 7: 322.

[40] Perhaps it would have been more consistent with Kant's view of animals if he had said that the soon-to-be humans in the state of nature did not possess the capacity for means-end reasoning, in the same way as other animals do not, in Kant's view, fully possess it.

of human history – cultivation, civilization, and moralization – that Kant discusses in the third *Critique*, in the "Universal History" essay, and in several other places. Before the first use of reason, the soon-to-be human presumably had not even entered into the first phase of human history, the cultivation of reason, since this phase requires the use of reason. In *Lectures of Pedagogy*, for example, Kant characterizes cultivation as "the procurement of skillfulness . . . [which] is the possession of a faculty which is sufficient for the carrying out of whatever purpose."[41] The first use of reason depicted in "Conjectural Beginning" can be therefore understood as the beginning of the stage of the cultivation of reason – a stage that comes before the other two.

However, this attribution is contentious, too. The technical predisposition in the human being and the ability to act in accordance with the technical hypothetical imperative are often associated with the creation of art and science, and thus with the cultivation of reason.[42] Kant talks about cultivation as the process of learning skillfulness of carrying out an end by finding suitable means, but without yet being able to set an end for oneself (LP 9: 450). If this is so, then we could perhaps describe the primitive technical skills that the soon-to-be humans from "Conjectural Beginning" possessed even before their first use of reason as a part of the process of humanity's (early) cultivation.

The story of the first use of reason in "Conjectural Beginning" can also be articulated in the terms Kant uses in *Religion* to describe the three "elements of determination of the human being" or features of human nature, which are: "1. The predisposition to the *animality* of the human being, as a *living* being; 2. To the *humanity* in him, as a living and at the same time *rational* being; 3. To his *personality*, as a rational and at the same time *responsible* being."[43] The first predisposition, animality, is further characterized as a predisposition for which reason is *not* required and one that consists of the drives for self-preservation, for the propagation of the species, and for co-existence with others.[44] Even though in *Religion* we find no suggestion about the chronological nature of learning to exercise these predispositions, we might understand them in this way in light of "Conjectural Beginning" (and Kant's remarks about the progress of reason in his lectures of anthropology). This is because his characterization of the predisposition to animality in *Religion* comes very close to what he says about the soon-to-be humans in the state of nature in "Conjectural Beginning." There, these individuals are also incapable of using reason and are also in possession of instincts that allow them to survive and procreate.[45]

---

[41] Ped, 9: 450.   [42] See, for example, CJ, 5: 293, 5: 306, Anth, 7: 322, Ped, 9: 450.

[43] Rel, 6: 26.   [44] Rel, 6: 26–27.

[45] One point of difference is that "Conjectural Beginning," presenting a story about a human couple, does not emphasize the social drive this early on in human development. This interesting

Looking at the *Religion* passage about our three predispositions in light of the story of the first humans in "Conjectural Beginning," we see that the characterization of our species through these three predispositions in *Religion* may have a temporal aspect to it. First, we could only exercise the predisposition to animality, for which reason does not have to be used and which match the picture of the soon-to-be humans in the state of nature when they belong solely to the animal kingdom. Second, after the first active employment of reason, we could exercise the predisposition to humanity and prudential thinking. And, third, we have been and still are continuously learning to be moral and responsible (i.e., to exercise our predisposition to personality).

Having articulated Kant's speculative account of the first use of reason in terms familiar from his critical philosophy, I return to the story presented in "Conjectural Beginning" and to the four steps of reason's awakening. After the first step of humankind's emancipation from the state of nature, which – as we have seen – consisted in discovering the faculty of free choice (reason), Kant sketches three further ones. The second step consists in the human's realization that he can manipulate the desires of the human being in order to dominate others.[46] (Here Kant echoes Rousseau's second *Discourse* once again.) Unlike the first step, which challenged the instinct of nourishment, the second step challenges the sexual instinct.

The human being learns to exercise power over the other human by prolonging and provoking the other human's sexual drive with the use of the biblical fig leaf.[47] The third step of reason's awakening consists in the human's newly emerged concern for his future and, in particular, realization that the future will bring many challenges and hardships.[48]

In the fourth and final step, the human "comprehended (however obscurely) that he was the genuine end of nature, and that in this nothing that lives on earth can supply a competitor for him."[49] This step is crucial because it consists in the realization that we are distinct from the other species and do not solely belong to the animal kingdom. It also involves the realization that we are equal to other human beings but not equal to other animals. Through this fourth step of reason's awakening, Kant hints at the fact that the first humans must have had

---

difference can be attributed to Kant's heavy reliance on the story of the Garden of Eden from Genesis. But we find the mention of our social drive elsewhere: in the anthropology lectures, where Kant does not choose to rely on Genesis, he indeed suggests that our drive for social life forms a part of our animal nature (Anth-Mron, 25: 1416).

[46] CB, 8: 112–13.

[47] For a feminist interpretation of the Kantian rendition of the first human's sexual awakening, see Zimmer 2022.

[48] CB, 8: 113–14.   [49] CB, 8: 114.

some – however crude and undeveloped – capacity for moral thinking and thus positive freedom:

> The first time he [the new human] said to the sheep: Nature has given you the skin you wear not for you but for me, then took it off the sheep and put it on himself (Genesis 3:21), he became aware of a prerogative that he had by his nature over all animals . . . . *This representation includes (however obscurely) the thought of the opposite: that he must not say something like this to any human being, but has to regard him as an equal participant in the gifts of nature – a preparation from afar for the restrictions that reason was to lay on the will in the future in regard to his fellow human beings*, and which far more than inclination and love is necessary to the establishment of society. *And thus the human being had entered into an equality with all rational beings*, of whatever rank they might be (Genesis 3:22); namely, in regard to the claim of being himself an end, of also being esteemed as such by everyone else, and *of being used by no one merely as a means to other ends.*[50]

This passage, described by Yovel as one where "[m]an's actual humanization is . . . achieved,"[51] shows that Kant's conjectural account of reason's emergence is intended to be compatible with his transcendental account of freedom at least with respect to the idea that the ability to choose beyond natural determination entails a basic moral awareness. In its crude and undeveloped version from the "Conjectural Beginning," this moral awareness amounts to (1) an awareness that the human has "a prerogative" over other living beings and (2) that the human must regard other humans as "equal participant[s] in the gifts of nature" or that he has an moral equal status as all other rational beings. Kant hastens to note that only the first thought – that the human has "a prerogative" over other, non-human living beings – is a clear one. The second thought – that the human must regard other humans as "equal participant[s] in the gifts of nature" – is an obscure thought that only constitutes "a *preparation from afar* for the restrictions that reason was to lay on the will *in the future* in regard to his fellow human beings." He is suggesting here that the newly emerged moral awareness or capacity for moral action will only be properly exercised by the human beings in years to come.[52] For now, the moral awareness is not something the human being will actually act on (even though he, theoretically speaking, could act on it). This is why the first use of reason, choosing to eat from the tree of

---

[50] CB, 8: 114, emphasis added.   [51] Yovel 1989, 192.

[52] This point is well illustrated by Barbara Herman, who notes: "the metaphysical fact of the freedom of the will is not sufficient for our being or becoming fully moral persons, for our being *moralized* . . . . That is, for a human being to be a moral person requires her having some specific non-metaphysical abilities, and, Kant's argument might be, *these* abilities require the setting of civil society for their development" (Herman 2009, 158). Herman wrote this in the context of "Universal History," but her remark is equally relevant to "Conjectural Beginning."

knowledge, consisted merely in exercising the pragmatic capacity of reason, not the moral one. We here witness a mythical beginning of the slow moral progress of our species – a progress with regard to how often and how consistently we act from the moral law – toward which we will strive for millennia to come. As Yovel aptly puts it, "with the end of the pre-history of reason, its history proper only begins."[53]

1.2.4 The Human Being as a Unique Member of the Animal Kingdom

Once reason awoke and emancipated the human being from the tutelage of nature, the uniqueness of our species within the animal kingdom became clear.[54] The principal and overarching reason for this uniqueness is, of course, that the human being is the only animal that belongs not only to the system of nature (the animal kingdom), but also to the "world system"[55] or the "rational" and "spiritual" kingdom.[56] By virtue of belonging to these two realms instead of solely to the realm of nature, we are able to manipulate and surpass our animalistic instincts, acting freely from them. In other words, we are able to think and act independently from the causal laws of nature. This is because we are capable of manipulating things (technical predisposition) and of creating culture and developing unequal relations with others of our kind (pragmatic predisposition).[57]

Non-human animals fully rely on their natural instincts and, as a result, do not have to train and teach their offspring anything they need for their survival and happiness. They also do not have to take care of them beyond a short period after their birth. But the human being – who creates, builds, and invents things useful to him – requires being trained and taught by other people, and requires a longer period of time during which he is under their care and nourishment.[58] The human being is the only animal who needs certain external factors, such as appropriate education and political institutions, to develop his natural propensities and to improve his nature: "Every animal already knows through instinct what it has to do . . . . The main difference with human beings is that they must be taught."[59] Given that one's education and formation necessarily require the input of other human beings, it comes as no surprise that Kant emphatically states that the human being cannot develop his predispositions and reach his vocation by himself, but only in a social setting.[60] I will return to this topic in Section 2.

---

[53] Yovel 1989, 193.

[54] I say *fully* evident because even before the first use of reason our species was in some ways special and distinct from any other one in their physical characteristics, social drive, and primitive technical abilities that could be passed across generations. Moreover, before reason's awakening this faculty had presumably been dormant, not non-existing.

[55] Anth-Mron, 25: 1415.   [56] Anth-Mron, 25: 1420.   [57] Anth, 7: 323.   [58] Ped, 9: 441–51.

[59] Anth-Mron, 25: 1416–17.   [60] IUH, 8: 18–19, Anth, 7: 324, Ped, 9: 441–51.

While the fact of our belonging to both the animal kingdom and the spiritual kingdom is well known in Kantian scholarship, it will be valuable to explore the ways in which this fact is discussed in the anthropological context. In the Friedländer transcription of Kant's 1775–76 lectures on anthropology, he states that "[the] human being has two determinations [*Bestimmungen*], one with regard to humanity, and one with regard to animality."[61] In the later Mrongovious transcription of his 1784–85 lectures, he similarly says: "Here we have only spoken of the animal determination [*Bestimmung*] of the human being. But now we must speak also of the spiritual determination [*Bestimmung*] of the human being."[62] In Friedländer, as in the transcriptions of his later lectures – Menschenkunde (1781–82) and Mrongovious (1784–85) – what immediately follows the remark about our dual nature is the observation that our humanity and animality are fundamentally in *conflict*.[63] To achieve the perfection of humanity, we would have to "do violence" to our animality.[64]

But the fundamental conflict between our two determinations is a productive one. As we read in Mrongovious, "this opposition between the animal and spiritual nature of the human being itself ultimately contributes to the production of the final destiny of the human being."[65] In Menschenkunde we find a similar thought: "animality and freedom . . . are the sources of the incentives of everything evil and the origin thereof."[66] This thought is echoed frequently in Kant's writings whenever he discusses his vision of humanity's progress. What Kant means is that the effects of our freedom of thought and action – gradual socialization and creation of culture – inflame our animalistic desires and inclinations, developing ever more unrealistic and overblown needs whose fulfillment requires competing with other people for social status, power, and natural resources. This opposition between our animal and spiritual determination is fundamentally about our relation to other humans, and is well known under the term "unsociable sociability" from "Universal History." This term is introduced in the Fourth Proposition and is characterized in the following way:

> The human being has an inclination to become *socialized*, since in such a condition he feels himself as more a human being, i.e. feels the development of his natural predispositions. But he also has a great propensity to *individualize* (isolate) himself, because he simultaneously encounters in himself the

---

[61] Anth-Fried, 25: 682.

[62] Anth-Mron, 25: 1420. It is interesting that he uses the word *Bestimmung*, usually translated as "vocation," in these two contexts to denote both our humanity and our animality, even though this term is more often reserved for the former – the "human vocation" – and conveys the idea of gradual fulfillment or development.

[63] Anth-Fried, 25: 682, Anth-Mensch, 25: 1199, Anth-Mron, 25: 1420.

[64] Anth-Fried, 25: 682. [65] Anth-Mron, 25: 1420. [66] Me 25: 1199.

unsociable property of willing to direct everything so as to get his own way and hence expects resistance everywhere.[67]

Unsociable sociability is the feature of our nature that describes the unique relationship we have toward living in the condition of sociality. It is responsible for our capacity for forming comparative judgments: assessing our wellbeing and our needs in light of what others have.[68] It is exactly what Kant hints at when he answers the question "Is the human being created for society or not?" in the Mrongovious anthropology lectures by saying:

> The human being is not created for the hive like the bees, but he is also not placed in the world as a solitary animal; rather, on the one hand, he has a propensity toward society due to his needs, which are far greater for him than for the animals. On the other hand, the human being also has a principle toward unsociability, for a society that is too large limits and discomforts him, and forces him to be on his guard.[69]

(These lectures were given in the same year that Kant published the "Universal History" essay where he explicitly formulates the term "unsociable sociability.")

In the Menschenkunde lectures on anthropology Kant even hints at the thought that prior to the awakening of reason, our nature could not have been characterized by the principle of unsociable sociability. The second element of this term, sociability – the drive to live in a social condition – was simply not a part of our psychology: "In the crude condition [the state of nature] a great unsociability also takes place with the human being, which springs from fear, a fear which prevails over each person within; hence the point in time when the talents of the human being can properly develop actually only arises in a civil constitution."[70] The awakening of reason and becoming humans proper, depicted speculatively in the "Conjectural Beginning," put into action unsociable sociability – nature's means of ensuring the development of our predispositions. The entrance into sociality and frequent interactions with others thus caused the reliance on others when it comes to one's assessment of one's worth and happiness. The fact that what characterizes prehistorical humans in the state of nature is a simple unsociability, as the quotefrom Menschenkunde suggests, stands in conflict with Wood's suggestion that human sociability belongs to our predisposition to animality, while our unsociability to our predisposition to humanity.[71]

---

[67] IUH, 8: 20–21. For extensive studies of the concept of unsociable sociability, see Schneewind 2009 and Wood 2009.

[68] Anth-Mron, 25: 1422.   [69] Anth-Mron, 25: 1416.   [70] Me 25: 1199.

[71] Wood writes: "Unsociable sociability is, to begin with, a modification of human *sociability* that belongs, along with our instincts for survival and reproduction, to our original natural predisposition to *animality*. ... The *unsociable* form taken by the sociability of human beings is not a consequence of our animality, but rather of our predisposition to *humanity*" (Wood 2009, 115).

1.3 Reason's Trajectory: From Selfishness to Morality

In the previous section, I have reconstructed Kant's speculative remarks about our species' prehistorical existence as animals and his story of the transition that our species underwent from mere irrational animals into primitive humans who can use reason. This section will present my reading of Kant's teleological account of humankind's gradual rational progress – that is, of the further stages of the progress of human reason. I will also show how the story of humankind's beginning fits with his broader view of human history as such.

This section is organized as follows. In Section 1.3.1, I discuss the way in which the first use of reason awakened in us the propensity to evil and self-interested tendencies. The realization that desires can be manipulated prompted humans to enter into the condition of sociality for self-interested purposes: so that we can inflict injustice on others and use them to satisfy our own desires. Here I draw primarily on "Universal History" and "Conjectural Beginning." In Section 1.3.2 I show how our motivational psychology is supposed to develop and change alongside the gradual improvement of the rules that govern our social order. The change in our motivational psychology can be described as a slow attempt to become enlightened or to adopt a "pluralistic" standpoint of reason – the standpoint of assuming one's coexistence in a *community* with others (as citizens of the world), and of regarding oneself as governed by the universal law which governs the pursuit of everyone's conceptions of happiness.[72] I also discuss the three means by which this progress can happen: education, legislation, and religion. I conclude in Section 1.3.3 by briefly discussing the ways in which Kant's speculative account of humankind's beginning fits together with his teleological view of human history.

1.3.1 Reason's Egoism

According to Kant's conjectural story of humankind's beginning in the "Conjectural Beginning," the initial use of reason for setting ends that go beyond nature had enormous consequences for our species' further development. Most immediately, it was the cause of our feeling discontent for the first time and of the development of a vicious side of humans: the "evil" that hence became a part of our nature.[73] This happened, Kant speculates, because the pleasant feeling of being superior to other living beings that are unable freely to choose their desires and act independently of their instinct was soon replaced by the negative feelings of "anxiety and fright . . . concerning how he [the human being] . . . should deal with this newly discovered faculty. He stood, as it were,

---

[72] Anth, 7: 130.　[73] CB, 8: 119.

on the brink of an abyss."[74] From there, the realization that particular desires can be controlled (increased, decreased, or changed altogether) led to the emergence of evil desires, such as the desire to be comparatively better off than others around one and to gain control over others; these, as I will show, led to the development of unequal and unjust social relations.

Kant's anthropological view of evil implies that the first occurrences of evil coincided (non-incidentally) with the entrance into the condition of sociality. Within the condition of sociality, the human being saw himself as having to pay attention to others because they posed, or at least could potentially pose, a threat to the realization of his own desires and needs. Moreover, paying attention to others resulted in the emergence of comparative judgments and competitive inclinations, which led to evil intentions and actions. My interpretation of the Kantian conception of human evil is thus compatible with Allen Wood's, according to whom the evil that humans are capable of "pertain[s] to us insofar as we are social beings" and is "closely bound up with our tendencies to compare ourselves with others and compete with them for self-worth."[75]

Wood's claim that, for Kant, the condition of sociality is the source and the necessary condition of humans' evil actions[76] has been challenged by Jeanine Grenberg. Grenberg claims that there are certain types of evil actions that can be committed without interaction with other humans.[77] Moreover, she understands "the condition of sociality" in *moral* terms: "the social for Kant is thus the realm within which we share specifically moral purposes with other persons."[78] However, I disagree with Grenberg on these two points, in favor of Wood's interpretation of Kantian evil. Firstly, Kant's anthropological account of the historical emergence and evolution of our practical capacities shows that our moral capacities in general emerged *after* the entrance into the condition of sociality (see Section 1.2.3). Therefore, we cannot define the notion of sociality in moral terms, since we enter the condition of sociality significantly *before* we develop our moral capacities, which is a lengthy process spanning many generations. Secondly, while Grenberg is right to claim that it is not the case that any evil action is only possible in a situation of sociality, it is the case, for Kant, that sociality was a necessary condition for the emergence of the very possibility of moral wrongdoing. Rational evil emerges when people begin social interactions beyond those intended for procreation and for securing the survival of the individual and the species: the entrance into the condition of sociality conditions the emergence of the capacity for moral evil. Thus Grenberg's argument against Wood's claim that the condition of sociality is

---

[74] CB, 8: 112.   [75] Wood 1999, 287.   [76] Wood 1991, 1999.   [77] Grenberg 2009, 182–94.
[78] Grenberg 2009, 186.

the source and the necessary condition of humans' evil actions seems misguided because it overlooks Kant's historical-anthropological account of the development of our practical rational capacities.

This interpretation of the Kantian evil poses the question about the moral responsibility for the evil humans caused at the earliest stages of our species' development: given that this evil took place before the proper development of our moral capacities, can Kant maintain (as he does elsewhere) that early humans were responsible for their wrong actions? To answer this question, I return to a crucial passage from "Conjectural Beginning" quoted in Section 1.2.3 (at 8: 114). In this passage, Kant claims that the first act of using an animal for one's own purposes carried with it simultaneously the (however crude) realization that another human being cannot be used in this way because of the fundamental equality shared by all human beings (an equality that animals, by contrast, do not share with humans). This realization, Kant goes on to suggest, amounted to an obscure awareness that all human beings are ends in themselves and are not to be used as means to other ends. Kant thus believes that even the early humans must have had some primitive capacity for moral thinking and thus positive freedom. Given this, he can also coherently maintain that they were morally responsible for their evil actions. That the proper development of our moral capacities was to take place in later stages of human history does not mean that these capacities were not present at all early on, nor does it mean they were not responsible for their evil actions. Rather, it means that early humans had less socio-political and educational resources to develop their moral character and hence that regularly conforming to the moral law – being morally virtuous – was more challenging for them. Kant's account of reason's development tells us not how morality is created at some point in time, but how moral demands and principles gradually become fully *understood* by humans – a phenomenon that is, as Kleingeld reminds us, compatible with the timeless and universal validity of the moral law.[79]

The conceptual relation between the evil in our nature and the gradual development of our predispositions can be understood in the following way. Sociality is a condition for the very possibility of human, as opposed to purely animal, development.[80] However, human sociality necessarily involves unsociable sociability, from which all kinds of evil are derived. Nevertheless, unsociable sociability (being a condition of human development) is also the condition for the development of the goods of human life, such as the sciences and the arts. As Schneewind puts it, "The energies we devote to showing others how much stronger and smarter we are lead us to create ingenious inventions and brilliant

---

[79] Kleingeld 1999, 65–69.   [80] Recall Me 25: 1199.

new ideas that gradually enrich and enlighten our strife-ridden common lives."[81] Therefore, as Kant argues in "Universal History," a just political order is needed in order to have these goods while minimizing the evils of unsociable sociability (such as greed, competition, and envy). The evolution of our juridical order is driven by the need to minimize the extent to which we are motivated by our propensity to evil – and so by the very existence of evil.

These ideas also echo Rousseau's second *Discourse* (itself a conjectural account of the origins of sociality and morality). According to Rousseau, when our species existed within the state of nature, everyone was independent from one another and all of our needs were satisfied. This happiness and independence ceased after the human being exited the state of nature and entered a preliminary condition of civility. This made us timid, feeble, and servile.[82] In particular, we developed new, excessive desires that could only be satisfied with the help of others, and, due to commodities that they enjoyed by living in small groups with others, we became dependent on other human beings.[83] Rousseau effectively claims that, in Schneewind's words, "sociability develops with a vengeance: the struggle for social distinction makes us slaves to our need to impress others in whatever ways we can."[84] According to Rousseau, moreover, the entrance into the condition of sociality or civility was the first step towards inequality among humans because it provoked interpersonal comparisons, jealousy, shame, and the importance of public esteem. People became greedy and competitive, and thus started trying to use others for their own purposes.[85] This picture closely resembles Kant's vision of the initial condition of sociality that led to the emergence of new – self-interested – desires correlated with comparative judgments and to the treatment of others as means to one's ends. Furthermore, according to Rousseau (as well as Kant), the direct cause of the development of egoism in the human being was man's realization that the species he belongs to is better and more important than other species.[86] This, of course, is reiterated by Kant in the "Conjectural Beginning" essay.[87] Finally, Kant's view from the "Conjectural Beginning" that non-human animals, by contrast with human beings, are limited to their natural instincts and thus do not have free will, can also be traced back to Rousseau, who claims: "while nature alone activates everything in the operations of a beast, man participates in his own actions in his capacity as a free agent. The beast chooses

---

[81] Schneewind 2009, 94.   [82] *Discourse*, 86.

[83] Rousseau writes: "it is impossible to enslave a man without first putting him in a situation where he cannot do without another man, and since such a situation does not exist in the state of nature, each man there is free of the yoke, and the law of the strongest is rendered vain" (*Discourse*, 106).

[84] Schneewind 2009, 102.   [85] *Discourse*, 116–22.   [86] *Discourse*, 110.   [87] CB, 8: 112.

or rejects by instinct, man by an act of free will. ... Nature commands all animals, and the beast obeys. Man receives the same impulsion, but he recognizes himself as being free to acquiesce or resist."[88]

But Kant's account of human nature is more positive in the main than Rousseau's account. According to Kant, our propensity to evil is not just the cause of numerous bad things that happened to mankind, but also the indirect cause of everything good. In Yovel's words, "it is not by renouncing reason but by the power of reason itself that its ills and conflicts with nature are to be finally resolved."[89] Most importantly, our propensity to evil has an indirect impact on the gradual development of the juridical order, whose rules, however unjust initially, slowly develop into ever more just and egalitarian ones. As Guyer puts it, "Human beings living in close contact with one another will apparently be forced by mere prudence to discover and adhere to just laws."[90] The gradual improvement of our juridical order results from minimizing our unsociable sociability, and this happens because we realize that a lawful condition will protect our individual self-interests.[91] However, as Deligiorgi points out, the establishment of a just constitution does not require a complete eradication of this antagonism.[92] We may perhaps think of the regulative ideal of establishing an ethical community composed of perfectly moral citizens (see Section 1.3.2) as synonymous with a complete eradication of unsociable sociability from our nature (which, of course, can never actually happen). The progressive development of social relations, therefore, is closely connected to the attempts to minimize the evil individuals are capable of via socio-political means – attempts that, however, are motivated by individuals' self-interest and competitiveness, not by considerations of the well-being of others. The phenomenon of unsociable sociability can be also observed at the level of international relations: while national self-interests drive individual states to war, their interest in commerce and trade lead them to the gradual establishment of peaceful relations.[93]

As Kant writes in "Universal History," "Thanks be to nature ... for the incompatibility, for the spiteful competitive vanity, for the insatiable desire to possess or even to dominate! For without them all the excellent natural predispositions in humanity would eternally slumber undeveloped."[94] Without unsociable sociability and competition between human beings, the development of the arts, sciences, or any complex rationality at all (including moral rationality) would not take place. But even though unsociable sociability can indirectly lead to a just juridical state, this passage makes it clear that before such a state can be established, unsociable sociability leads to gross and terrible inequalities and

---

[88] *Discourse*, 87–88.   [89] Yovel 1989, 194.   [90] Guyer 2009, 132.
[91] IUH, 8: 28, TPP, 8: 348.   [92] Deligiorgi, 2017, 697–98.   [93] IUH, 8: 24–26, TPP, 8: 361.
[94] IUH, 8: 21.

injustices between people – a situation that can only be solved by establishing just rules of conduct. Despite the general progressive character of our sociopolitical development, this development is not exactly a straightforward, linear process. As Louden writes, "On Kant's view, humans are by no means causally determined to achieve unilinear cultural progress. Rather, we pursue progress as free beings who can and do change our minds. Cultural regress and nonprogressive cultural change are thus always present as distinct possibilities."[95]

When in the "Conjectural Beginning" Kant (similarly to Rousseau) describes the first use of reason and the resulting activation of our propensity to evil as well as the tendency to compete with others for self-worth, he seems to be suggesting that the standpoint of an individual who has just entered into the condition of sociality – of an individual who uses reason to create new desires and find means to satisfy them – is *self-interested*, for such an individual is not capable of considering his own desires as on a par with the desires of others. Without fully fledged sociality, the individual portrayed in the "Conjectural Beginning" is not able to have a clear understanding that other human beings are his equals, but only an obscure one (see Section 1.2.3). As both "Universal History" and "Conjectural Beginning" suggest, every human being, having noticed the egoism of his companions and having suffered from anxiety and fright concerning his future, was inclined to set up regulations or laws that enforce just and fair behavior, so that the self-interested others do not impede the realization of his goals and desires.[96] Kant suggests therefore that humans entered the condition of sociality for self-interested reasons, since sociality started with self-interested and competitive individuals who wanted to exploit others to satisfy their own ends. Specifically, the original reasons for setting up and developing sociopolitical arrangements and a juridical order, caused by nonrational emotions such as anxiety as well as by increasing knowledge about the capacities of others, were self-interested.

The first use of reason exercised by an individual who on the brink of exiting the state of nature, therefore, led the human being to become what Kant calls in the *Anthropology* a "practical egoist": someone who

> limits all ends to himself, sees no use in anything except that which is useful to himself, and . . . puts the supreme determining ground of his will simply in utility and his own happiness, not in the thought of duty. For, since every

---

[95] Louden 2017, 720–1; see also Kant's *Conflict of the Faculties*, 7:87.

[96] On the picture I am sketching here concerning the "Universal History," it is *not* the case that one's realization that other people's wills conflict with my own straightforwardly amounts to achieving a capacity for moral reasoning. On my picture, the realization that other people's wills conflict with my own will is initially used only for egoistic purposes (rational egoism); this takes place (temporally speaking) much before our species attains the very capacity for moral reasoning.

other human being also forms his own different concept of what he counts as happiness, it is precisely egoism which drives him to have no touchstone at all of the genuine concept of duty, which absolutely must be a universally valid principle.[97]

Kant's anthropological description of the practical egoist suggests that such a person acts solely in accordance with the technical-hypothetical imperative (he "sees no use in anything except that which is useful to himself") *and* the pragmatic-hypothetical imperative (he "puts the supreme determining ground of his will simply in utility and his own happiness"), but *not* in accordance with the categorical imperative. The practical egoist knows which means will satisfy which goals and is capable of determining or pursuing his own happiness. (While this term can be used to describe the mental capacities of the human being right after his first use of reason, it can also be used to describe a morally blameworthy individual in a more advanced society.) However, Kant suggests, the practical egoist does not regard himself as a citizen of the world [*Weltbürger*] or as a member of a community of all human beings in which every member is subject to the same law.[98] The concept of happiness is not universally valid since every person can decide for himself what counts as happiness; by, contrast, the concept of duty is universally valid (the same for everyone), but to comprehend it would require seeing things from other people's standpoints.

1.3.2 Reason's Gradual Development

The picture that emerges from "Universal History" and "Conjectural Beginning" is that the first use of reason led the human being to enter into the condition of sociality, and this in turn led to his becoming a practical egoist. However, as "Universal History" goes on to explain, reason was not just the cause of this one feature of our moral psychology: once appropriately developed, reason can be also used to guide us to minimize our competitiveness and the evil in our nature. Living in the social condition first makes us rational, competitive, and self-interested, but it can eventually, through appropriate political and institutional arrangements, resolve the problems created by unsocial sociability and thus *change* our way of perceiving one another.[99]

---

[97] Anth, 7: 130. In the same section from the *Anthropology* (7: 128–30), Kant distinguishes three types of egoism: logical egoism (when one "considers it unnecessary to test his judgment also by the understanding of others"), aesthetic egoism (when one "is satisfied with his own taste, even if others . . . criticize or even laugh at [it]"), and practical egoism. The terms "practical egoist" and "practical egoism" do not appear in Kant's writings before *Anthropology*.

[98] Anth, 7: 130.   [99] IUH, 8: 23–28, TPP, 8: 666–67.

As Philip Kain has argued, referencing "Universal History" and *Perpetual Peace*, self-interest, conflict, and war slowly lead toward the same end that moral reflection would have dictated if it governed our actions from the beginning of humankind.[100] However, Kain has failed to observe that "Conjectural Beginning" is also a text worth discussing in this context, as it contains valuable remarks about the way in which conflict leads to gradual moralization.[101] Kant writes:

> [C]ulture must proceed in order properly to develop the predispositions of humanity as a moral species to their vocation, so that the latter no longer conflict with humanity as a natural species. From this conflict . . . arise all true ills that oppress human life, and all vices that dishonor it; nevertheless, the incitements to the latter, which one blames for them, are in themselves good and purposive as natural predispositions, but these predispositions, since they were aimed at the merely natural condition, suffer injury from progressing culture and injure culture in turn, until perfect art again becomes nature, which is the ultimate goal of the moral vocation of the human species.[102]

The progress of the human being and humanity as a whole can be described as consisting in eliminating within oneself the standpoint of a practical egoist (discussed in Section 1.3.1) and striving to adopt the opposite standpoint – that of an enlightened individual[103] or, as Kant puts it in the *Anthropology*, of a "pluralist."[104] The progress of any individual, as we have seen, requires the help of others and the existence of appropriate institutional structures. More specifically, there are three means to human progress: education, legislation, and religion,[105] education being perhaps the most important and fundamental one.[106] These three ways of one's rational and moral progress, as I will show here, all emphasize the need to regard and conduct oneself as a citizen of the world [*Weltbürger*]. Of course, while legal and political arrangements can only teach us to behave in conformity with the law, the step to begin obeying the law for the sake of it is a step each individual has to decide to take for himself. The institutional (legal, educational, religious) arrangements in place are supposed only to *aid* each individual in making this choice. Education, moreover, can

---

[100] Kain 1989, 331.   [101] CB, 8: 115–18.   [102] CB, 8: 117–18.

[103] In the essay "An Answer to the Question: What Is Enlightenment?" (1784), notably written around the same time as "Universal History," Kant defines the condition of enlightenment as "man's emergence from his self-incurred immaturity [or tutelage]" (WE 8: 40), that is, emergence from the inability to use one's understanding without someone else's help due to lack of resolution or courage.

[104] Anth, 7: 130.   [105] Anth-Mensch, 25: 1198, Anth-Mron, 25: 1427.

[106] In the Mrongovious transcription of Kant's lectures on anthropology he states: "In the end we will perhaps see that, concerning the well-being of the world, everything depends on education" (Anth-Mron, 25: 1428). In *Lectures on Pedagogy* he similarly remarks: "The human being can only become human through education" (LP 9: 443).

provide us with materials for maxims, give us examples of virtuous actions, and make us realize the importance of moral resolution.[107] As Yovel notes, nature can further human progress "only in the external sphere of legality; it can also remove external obstacles to the spread of morality; but it cannot contribute anything to the creation of the moral-historical end itself."[108]

For Kant, the intellectual achievements of one generation are a baseline, as it were, for the education and development of the generation that is to follow. The maturing of people from the next generation depends on how enlightened the individuals in public roles – especially teachers, political leaders, and religious leaders – currently are. This is why "the correct concept of the manner of education can only arise if each generation transmits its experience and knowledge to the next, each in turn adding something before handing it over to the next."[109] If a critical number of generations succeeds in this regard, then "education will get better and better and each generation will move one step closer to the perfection of humanity."[110] For one generation collectively to take a step toward enlightenment, therefore, is a necessary condition of the enlightenment of individuals who will live in the future.

The role of the teachers, specifically, is to design and execute the right plan of education for the schools – a plan whose aim is to improve the human condition. Kant notes in the *Lectures on Pedagogy*:

> the design for a plan of education must be made in a *cosmopolitan* manner. . . . Accordingly, the set-up for the schools should depend entirely on the judgment of *the most enlightened experts.* . . . It is only through the efforts of people . . . who take an *interest* in the best world and who are capable of conceiving the idea of a future improved condition, that the gradual approach of human nature to its purpose is possible.[111]

The role of the teachers, Kant adds, is to promote not only technical skilfulness, but also to instil the ability to think in an enlightened way. The best teachers and other public figures try not only to develop the technical and prudential skills of the individuals under their governance, but also their morality, thus "bring[ing] posterity further than they themselves have gone."[112]

In addition to teachers, political leaders and religious authorities also play a key role in the maturing of the generation that follows them. The role of

---

[107] CPrR, 5: 153, MM, 6: 477–84.   [108] Yovel 1980, 185.   [109] Ped, 9: 446.

[110] Ped, 9: 444.

[111] Ped, 9: 448–89; my emphasis. In "Theory and Practice," Kant defines the cosmopolitan perspective as "a view to the well-being of the human race as a whole and insofar as it is conceived as progressing toward its well-being in the series of generations of all future times" (TP, 8: 277–78).

[112] Ped, 9: 449–50.

enlightened political leaders and the state in general is the protection of rightful freedom of its citizens. The state, for example, guards us against civil compulsion and compulsion over conscience.[113] It also ensures the freedom, equality, and independence of each of its citizens.[114] It thereby removes the obstacles to adopting the three maxims of good thinking – thinking for oneself, from the standpoint of others, and consistently – and encourages participation in the public domain and law-making. Here Kant's idea of a "moral politician" from the *Perpetual Peace* – of a leader whose political principles and decisions are compatible with morality[115] – can serve as an illustration of what kind of political leaders would be needed so that the country in question can progress toward enlightenment. The role of enlightened religious leaders, in turn, is to encourage their own and one another's moral progress and the cultivation of moral virtue, so that our behavior can transform from merely empirically good to intelligibly good (i.e., stemming from moral motives).

The development of the political, religious, and educational institutions and the development of our moral psychology are closely related. The disposition to practical egoism, which (as the "Conjectural Beginning" may suggest) characterized the first humans who started using reason, led to the emergence of an unjust juridical order, motivated by individual self-interest and competitiveness of its members. And, in the same way, the gradual improvement of our juridical order seems to be coupled with a psychological disposition that opposes practical egoism – a disposition Kant labels "pluralism": "The opposite of egoism can only be pluralism, that is, the way of thinking in which one is not concerned with oneself as the whole world, but rather regards and conducts oneself as a mere citizen of the world [*Weltbürger*]."[116] As a pluralist, Kant further explains, "[I would] have reason to assume, in addition to my own existence, the existence of a whole of other beings existing in community with me (called the world)."[117] On this anthropological picture, the pluralist – unlike the practical egoist – is capable of seeing things from other people's standpoints and of taking part in universally valid judgments (such as determining the concept of duty). These passages from the *Anthropology* suggest that a necessary condition for the existence of a juridical order composed of correctly motivated (not merely correctly behaving) people is that it consists of members who are "pluralists" in the Kantian sense, that is, who assume and accept their coexistence in a *community* with others (as citizens of the world), and hence regard themselves as governed by the universal, collectively and

---

[113] WOT, 8: 144–45.   [114] See, for example, TP, 8: 290–96 and WOT, 8: 144–45.

[115] TPP, 8: 372.   [116] Anth, 7: 130.

[117] Anth, 7: 130. But, Kant adds, the question whether I have such a reason belongs not to anthropology, but to metaphysics, and for this reason he does not pursue it further here.

unanimously agreed upon law that governs the pursuit of their conceptions of happiness.[118]

The definition of the pluralist from the *Anthropology* describes this individual as a *Weltbürger* – citizen of the world. This term is important for Kant's teleological view of humankind's progress. He does not only use it to describe what kind of standpoint of reason an individual should strive to achieve, but also to describe ideal political and juridical relations. Kant uses a cognate of this term in "Universal History" to define the ideal "cosmopolitan [*weltbürgerlicher*] condition" between states. As Kant writes in the Seventh Proposition, the condition of unsociable sociability among nations, "through destruction or at least dismemberment of all of [the nations] to form new bodies, . . . partly through the best possible arrangement of their civil constitution internally, partly through a common agreement and legislation externally" sets up a condition "which resembl[es] a civil commonwealth" (i.e., the condition of cosmopolitanism).[119] The notion of a cosmopolitan condition is then clarified in the Eighth Proposition, which focuses on connecting the development of our human predispositions to developing a perfect state constitution, where it is called "the womb in which all original predispositions of the human species will be developed."[120] Thus the Eighth Proposition explicitly connects the political condition of cosmopolitanism with the development of other predispositions of our species – including, we may add, the psychological standpoint of pluralism discussed in *Anthropology*. In *Anthropology*, Kant explicitly says that the gradual progress of our species is only possible by a progressive formation of all citizens of the world into a cosmopolitan system: "one cannot expect to reach the goal [of our species] by the free agreement of *individuals*, but only by a progressive organization of citizens of the earth into and toward the species as a system that is cosmopolitically united."[121] The right treatment of others within a large community – the *telos* of humankind's progress – has to be achieved via two separate, but mutually

---

[118] Kant's pluralism is not specifically a political notion, but an ethical one. I have at least two good reasons to interpret Kant's pluralism in moral terms. Firstly, pluralism gets defined in *Anthropology* as an attitude of "*regard[ing]* and *conduct[ing]* oneself as a mere citizen of the world." While the phrase "conducting oneself" typically refers to the way a person is behaving or acting (to an external phenomenon visible to others) regardless of the motives of such behaving, the phrase "regarding oneself" typically refers to the way a person is thinking about himself – in other words, to a genuine disposition which is assessable only by the agent himself. My second reason for interpreting Kant's pluralism in moral terms is that in the relevant passage from *Anthropology* pluralism (of a single type) is contrasted simultaneously with three types of egoism: logical, aesthetic, and practical or moral ("practical egoism" and "moral egoism" are synonymous for Kant is this passage). This juxtaposition suggests, I believe, that pluralism should be understood as a moral notion (contrasted with moral or practical egoism) and simultaneously as an aesthetic and a logical notion, which is contrasted with the other two types of egoism.

[119] IUH, 8: 25–26. See also CB, 8: 121, TPP, 8: 354–55.   [120] IUH, 8: 28.   [121] Anth, 7: 333.

reinforcing, processes: one internal (arriving at the disposition to *pluralism* within every human being) and one external (arriving at the political condition of *cosmopolitanism*).

Developing the political condition of cosmopolitanism is supposed to happen alongside the gradual moralization of its citizens, which, as Kant notes in "Universal History," would "transform a *pathologically* compelled agreement to form a society finally into a *moral* whole."[122] For Kant, forming the cosmopolitan condition is a necessary condition of people's achieving as virtuous a character as is humanely possible, just as forming individual states is a necessary condition of the beginning of our process of moralization. It would seem that a *pathologically* compelled agreement is the national jurid-ical order, while a *moral* whole would be a community of virtue (an "ethical state" in the terminology of the *Religion*), which perhaps aligns with the cosmopolitan condition. Such a community (also called an "ethical state" in direct contrast with the "juridico-civil state") would only need an ethical legislation (one that is freely accepted by all its members), not a coercive legislation.[123] The community of virtue would be composed of perfectly moral citizens who always choose to act on duty. This community is a regulative ideal that we must strive toward, even though we can never fully achieve it.[124] The rational development of our species, as Kleingeld puts it, "is ultimately to culminate in the self-transformation of society into a moral community."[125] At the very end of *Anthropology*, Kant similarly reminds us that, as he had already argued in "Universal History," human beings "feel destined by nature to develop, through mutual compulsion under laws that come from themselves, into a *cosmopolitan society*" – a progressive idea that "is only a regulative principle."[126] The idea of an infinite moral and political progress toward a successful formation of the ethical community or the cosmopolitan state is central to the idea of virtue. This progress can never be fully completed, however, because human beings will never be able to have a holy will devoid of any nonmoral inclinations.

Unfortunately, the relation between an ideal cosmopolitan condition (which would presumably require some coercive laws) and an ideal ethical community (which would not require them) does not emerge clearly from Kant's writings. The *Religion* expands Kant's ideas about the moral progress of a human community that we find in a more preliminary form in "Universal History." Unlike "Universal History," *Religion* (as well as "Doctrine of Virtue" from *Metaphysics of Morals*) are concerned with people's moral education and

---

[122] IUH, 8: 21. [123] Rel, 6: 94–95. [124] Rel, 6: 94–95. [125] Kleingeld 1999, 61.
[126] Anth, 7: 331. See also TPP, 8: 360–68.

development aside from political or legal means of furthering it[127]. *Religion* and *Metaphysics of Morals* do not draw a distinction between national state and cosmopolitan state when discussing the ethical community. It is thus unclear whether an ideal cosmopolitan state composed of pluralistically minded citizens needs juridical regulations – whether moralizing involves making a collective effort which is also a *political* effort. While "Universal History" and *Perpetual Peace* indeed suggest that moralizing involves a collective *political* effort, *Religion*, with its notion of the "ethical state," detaches the idea of collective moralizing from any political or juridical arrangements.[128]

1.3.3 The Beginning of Human History in Light of Its Later Stages

Having sketched Kant's view of human progress and of the gradual realization of human vocation, I want to conclude this Part of the Element by showing how it is complemented by the conjectural account of the beginning of human history, which I presented in Section 1.2.

When Kant speculates about the way we became rational in the distant past, he puts an emphasis on the new uncertainties that the newly emerged human being had to face once he realized he can think and act independently of nature's causal laws. Kant portrays this human being as faced with "anxiety and fright . . . concerning how he . . . should deal with this newly discovered faculty" and imaginatively depicts the position this human being is in as standing "on the brink of an abyss."[129] The human is uncertain about how to use reason in the right way. But because his reason is not a part of the natural world, he cannot rely on his innate instincts in order to know how to rightly use it. He also lacks training in this regard because he belongs, by assumption, to the first generation of rational human beings.

The history of humanity is, then, the history of learning how to exercise reason in the right way. Consequently, given the conflict between rationality and animality, the history of humanity is also the history of learning how to polish and tame our animality or "crudity."[130] To do so, the human being needs to

---

[127] These two works approach this issue differently. While *Religion* focuses on how to cultivate virtue, *Doctrine of Virtue* from *Metaphysics of Morals* focuses on what kind of virtues there are.

[128] In *Religion*, Kant envisions that the juridical state might eventually be transcended completely and an ethical state might emerge in its place. A juridical state is governed by coercive juridical laws, whereas an ethical state is governed by non-coercive laws of virtue alone. However, the connections between an ideal cosmopolitan order and an ideal ethical state are unclear in Kant's writings. In "Universal History," there is no idea of a universal religion of reason from the *Religion*. Instead, there is an idea of a world government, which requires forming a juridical state as well as further moralization. But this distinction is not made explicitly in this text. After "Universal History" of 1784, Kant develops the juridical-political line of thought in *Perpetual Peace* (1795) and the ethical-religious line of thought in *Religion* (1793), quite separately.

[129] CB, 8: 112.   [130] Ped, 9: 443.

slowly teach himself – and others around him – how to do this. Hence the human being "can only become human through education."[131] But this process of learning to exercise reason in the right way and to overcome natural inclinations is slow and gradual because it is filled with numerous failed attempts and mistaken choices.[132] Kant illustrates this point in "Universal History" by saying that the human being needs a "master" who will teach him how not to misuse his freedom and how to obey the universal law, but the only people who can perform such a role are other human beings who are in need of a master themselves.[133] Unlike in the case of other animals, then, realizing our human predispositions and becoming the best version of ourselves requires social, political, and pedagogical experiments: "With the human being, the species first reaches the destiny of humanity from generation to generation, since a generation always adds something to the enlightenment of the previous one."[134] It is impossible to learn to make a fully fledged, mature use reason in isolation from other humans or over a short period of time. This impossibility is already evident in the story of the first use of reason that begins human history from "Conjectural Beginning": the first use of reason does not bring any positive changes to the life of the individual who uses it; nor does it make evident how reason should be used to his benefit and the benefit of his species.

2 Kant's Conjectural History of Humanity's Beginning

2.1 Introduction

In this section of the Element, I zoom in on one particular text where the speculative account of the beginning of human history is presented in most detail: the "Conjectural Beginning of Human History." I first sketch an overview of the Enlightenment conjectural history genre (its origins and common characteristics) in Section 2.2. Then, in Section 2.2, I assess the ways in which Kant's "Conjectural Beginning" belongs to this genre as well as how distinct the "Conjectural Beginning" essay is from the most prominent and well-studied conjectural histories of the Enlightenment era, discussing the contribution that this essay has made to the conjectural history genre as a whole.

The latter question has been for the most part neglected in past and present studies of conjectural histories: the first ever theoretical discussion of this genre by Dugald Stewart (1854, 1858) and more recent articles and comprehensive studies on this genre[135] do not mention Kant's essay at all. By doing so, I fill in

---

[131] Ped, 9: 443.   [132] IUH, 8: 23, CB, 8: 123, Ped, 9: 451.   [133] IUH, 8: 23.
[134] Anth-Mron, 25: 1417.
[135] Höpfl 1987, Evnine 1993, Wolker 1995, Palmieri 2016, Santos Castro 2017, Smalligan Marušić 2017.

the gap in the existing historical scholarship on the conjectural history genre, thereby fostering a dialogue between Kant scholars and other intellectual historians of the Enlightenment era. I make room for this essay to both expand and challenge the boundaries of this genre whose theoretical establishment has thus far relied on other texts.

2.2 Conjectural Histories

The conjectural history genre emerged in the late seventeenth and early eighteenth century in response to a growing dissatisfaction with historiography or traditional history. Historiography was a way of writing about history that was aimed at the elites, focusing on major political events such as wars and conquests: "the chief task of traditional history [was] to record the 'truth for the instruction of mankind.' By 'truth,' however, sixteenth- and seventeenth-century British historians usually meant the warlike transactions of peoples' leaders or the peacetime deeds and accomplishments or kings, statesmen and legislators."[136] Historiography focused also on key historical figures known by name, and not on the everyday lives of ordinary people of different classes: "Traditional history considered that the 'public action' of remarkable personalities was the only subject worthy of the historian's attention."[137] The crisis that this genre reached reflected the need for composing historical accounts for a broader audience and focused on other, emerging social classes – a history where ordinary people could see themselves as actors. Accordingly, the newly emerging genre of conjectural history aimed at presenting typical lives of individuals and groups (not only elites) and focused on a variety of events these typical individuals might participate in (not just wars and conquests). Conjectural histories thus radically broke with the established tradition of historiography in several ways.

According to Robert Wokler, the first text that can be classified as a modern conjectural history is Samuel Pufendorf's *De jure naturae et gentium* of 1672.[138] In this work, which was regarded as the most important book of Enlightenment anthropology, Pufendorf provided a quintessential account of humans' passage from barbarism to civilization. He explained how we advanced from the savage state, in which our needs were easily satisfied, to a society of independent relations, in which our wants are more complex and require others' assistant for their fulfillment. He also claimed that, by creating ever more complex structures of communal life, humankind gradually parts ways from other species, being capable of improvement and creating culture.

---

[136] Santos Castro 2017, 159.   [137] Santos Castro 2017, 159.   [138] Wolker 1995, 36–37.

In other words, we are responsible for the creation of institutional arrangements that bind us.

For Frank Palmieri, the first full-length conjectural histories are two works from the 1720s: Giambattista Vico's *New Science* of 1725 and Bernard Mandeville's *Fable of Bees* of 1729. Vico presents history as the work of divine providence (a feature of his work which, as we will later see, goes against typical features of this genre) and appeals to providence to explain the course of nations. History, for him, does not take an unpredictable course, but a repetitive cyclical shape divided into three stages. Mandeville imagines that the fear of gods' power – of thunder, lightning, or other unseen powers – provoked a need in savage men to make sense of a threatening world. While he does not posit a set of distinct stages of human history, he "traces back from the known end point of government the periods for which no documentation existed, but through which human societies must have proceeded in order to reach recognizable political institutions."[139]

These early works written in the emerging conjectural history genre present us with a number of features that will later become typical for this genre. First of all, conjectural histories focus on the prehistorical existence of human beings which lies too far in the past for us to have any materials documenting this kind of life. In other words, conjectural histories trace the origins of society back to a time before the existence of any documents. According to the first theorist of this genre, the nineteenth-century Scottish philosopher Dugald Stewart, since we lack sufficient evidence about how life was developing in the prehistorical times, "we are under a necessity of supplying the place of fact by conjecture . . . [because] we are unable to ascertain how men have actually conducted themselves upon particular occasions, of considering in what manner they are likely to have proceeded, from the principles of their nature, and the circumstances of their external situation."[140] A paradigmatic conjectural history, Rousseau's *Discourse on Inequality*, focuses for instance on the earliest solitary human animal, before any civilization or sociality had emerged. In the *Natural History of Religion*, Hume similarly outlines the earliest stages of religious beliefs, beginning from animism.

This lack of available documents points to another key feature of this genre: its focus on the construction of plausible, albeit empirically unproven, conjectures and hypotheses about events in the far past. According to Stewart, the aim of conjectural history is not to discover how things actually happened, but merely showing how things might have gradually arisen in a natural way.[141]

---

[139] Palmieri 2016, 33.   [140] Stewart 1858, 33–34.
[141] Stewart 1858, 37; see also Smalligan Marušić 2017, 264.

Conjectural histories thus may be seen as inferences to the best explanation. In particular, conjectural histories constitute a paradigm for understanding human nature by attempting to explain, in broad strokes, how our species must have developed in order for the current political and cultural structures to have emerged. In the words of Smalligan Marušić, "Conjectural histories reveal the extent to which our present is 'counterfactually robust,' not in the sense that any particular individual would have acted in roughly the same way in roughly the same circumstances, but in the closely related sense that any sufficiently large community of people would have acted in roughly the same ways in roughly the same circumstances."[142] The unique epistemic status of the speculations present in conjectural histories and their distinctive temporality is evident from the use their authors make of a particular verb tense – the "conjectural necessary" form of the past. This tense is used to denote events that might have or must have taken place in the past given what we know about the past and the present. It differs from other grammatical ways of talking about the past (such as with the use of the simple past or past perfect tenses) because it does not denote what did take place, but what could have reasonably taken place. But it also differs from conditional claims about the past that describe counterfactuals because it does not describe past that is contrary to fact, but speculative past.[143] Conjectural histories do not purport to describe exactly what happened in the past and how life in society has evolved to take on its current form – they do not purport, in other words, to be empirically accurate. Nonetheless, they have a unique epistemic value and way of contributing to the body of knowledge regarding human nature: they fill in the space that is unoccupied by archeological and scientific findings because of the shortcomings of these empirical fields at the time when the conjectural history is being written. Conjectural histories thus present hypotheses drawn from inferences that can be formulated on the basis of sparse and inconclusive empirical data. Through its unique epistemology indicated by a unique use of grammatical tense, conjectural histories are a template for thinking about phenomena that are empirically underdetermined.

By positing stages of our species' social development, moreover, conjectural histories provide a way of organizing human history into a coherent whole composed of intelligible units. The delineation of several distinct and universal stages according to which human history developed in another paradigmatic feature of this genre. As Stewart writes, "it cannot fail to occur to us as an interesting question, by what gradual steps the transition has been made from the first simple efforts of uncultivated nature, to a state of things so wonderfully artificial and complicated."[144] This chain or series of universal transitional steps

---

[142] Smalligan Marušić 2017, 271.   [143] Palmieri 2016, 16.   [144] Stewart, 1858, 33.

between what Stuart calls 'rude tribes' and 'cultivated' society marks the progress of a society. The best-known example of such stages comes from Smith's *Wealth of Nations*, according to which humankind develops through a set of four stages based on four modes of subsistence: hunting and gathering, pasturage, agriculture, and commerce. Ferguson, in his *Essay on the History of Civil Society*, develops by contrast three successive stages: savage, barbarian, and civilized. Conjectural histories focused on more particular phenomena, such as Hume's *Natural History of Religion*, also frequently posit stages (in Hume's case, stages of religious belief: animism, polytheism, and monotheism). As Palmieri summarizes, historical stages depicted by conjectural historians "can be defined in terms of material or economic ways of life, forms of religious belief, accomplishments in science and technology, or phases in the life of an individual organism. ... Encompassing all these varieties, the concept of stages provides a way of thinking and organizing change and transformation from prehistory through historical times."[145] Relatedly, conjectural histories frequently assume that a specific event in time began human history (see, for example, Rousseau's second *Discourse*) and provide an explanation for, and posit circumstances of, humankind's exit from the state of nature.

According to conjectural historians, moreover, human behavior and the way it changes exhibit universal tendencies. This is related to their methodological choice of writing from a Euro-centric perspective and regarding European history as a norm for societal development. Stewart himself assumes that the social institutions and lifestyles that preceded modern European institutions are similar in certain aspects to the 'primitive tribes' that existed in other regions during that time.[146] He also theorizes that conjectural history is founded on the idea that human nature is both universal and sufficiently stable to enable the development of theories about the natural processes that gave rise to a particular phenomenon; this involves examining the external circumstances of a group of people in conjunction with the principles of human nature.[147] He writes, for example, "that the capacities of the human mind have been in all ages the same, and that the diversity of phenomena exhibited by our species is the result merely of the different circumstances in which men are placed."[148]

Another feature of conjectural histories is de-sanctification or a departure from biblical, providential accounts explaining human behavior and progress. Conjectural historians understand human nature as manufactured by mankind itself, not by God's creation or will. The human being is regarded as the author of his own world, shaped according to his own design, not in the image of God.

---

[145] Palmieri 2016, 46.　　[146] Smalligan Marušić 2017, 262.
[147] Stewart 1854a, 69–70; Stewart 1854b, vol. 3, 165.　　[148] Stewart 1858, iv.

Accordingly, the framework of Genesis, popular until the time of this genre's development, is abandoned. This abandonment takes on different forms. Rousseau (in the second *Discourse*), Hume (in the *Natural History of Religion*), and Smith (in the *Wealth of Nations*) set aside the biblical account and take religion fully out of their analysis. Condorcet (in the *Sketch for a Historical Picture*) and Mandeville (in the *Fable of Bees*), in turn, attack religious authority explicitly, taking a decisively anticlerical stance. In his *Ideas for a Philosophy of History of Mankind*, Herder recourses to a providential explanation to some extent, claiming that divinity implanted distinctive potentials in the various peoples, but overall casts his narrative in secular terms. According to Palmieri, "works in this genre place themselves in relation to a secularizing movement because of the nonprovidential framework they adopt: some actively press a critique of religion or an aggressive desacralizing; a few continue to use the language of providence; most participate quietly in the secularizing process."[149]

Conjectural historians also assume that the intentions of individuals and the actual consequences of their actions come apart, as a result of which large-scale organization emerges without human control. History happens without our knowing the course it will take, without human planning or foresight. In the *Wealth of Nations*, Smith famously argues that the pursuit of self-interest, through the mechanism that adjusts supply and demand, leads to everybody's benefit. Ferguson, in his *Essay on the History of Civil Society*, postulates that the first person who appropriated a piece of land did not expect to lay foundations for civil laws and political establishment; we might find a similar sentiment in Rousseau's second *Discourse*. The developmental story they present, Wolker claims, is not at all teleological; rather, "it is described in terms of the original sources that prompt it, not backward from its conclusion. It issues from the spring of human action, whose impetus is undirected by the supposed destiny of mankind's moral development."[150] Relatedly, conjectural historians believe that conflict and war play a big part in the conjectural explanation of the gradual progress of societies and laws. Conflict drives the human development forward by imposing ever new challenges and needs for redefining what a society is like.

The final characteristic of conjectural histories I want to draw attention to is that they exhibit ambivalent attitudes toward progress and the modern times. While writers such as Robertson, Kames, Millar, and Smith all advance the position that history is a narrative of progress, other writers such as Ferguson, Rousseau, and Hume complicate the picture of progressive historiography.[151] Ferguson, for example, pays attention to virtues distinctive of people in the

---

[149] Palmieri 2016, 41.   [150] Wolker 1995, 39.   [151] Palmieri 2016, 49–50.

stage of barbarism, which have been lost in the subsequent stage of civilization. For Ferguson and Hume, while the first transformation (from animism to polytheism, from savagery to barbarism) is an instance of improvement, the second one (from polytheism to monotheism, from barbarism to civilization) is more ambiguous and might even be reversible. Thus many conjectural historians view human progress as discontinuous and inconsistent.

2.3 Kant's "Conjectural Beginning" as a Conjectural History

Having provided a detailed characterization of conjectural histories with a particular emphasis on their paradigmatic features, I will now assess the ways in which Kant's "Conjectural Beginning" belongs to this genre as well as how distinct the "Conjectural Beginning" essay is from the most prominent and well-studied conjectural histories of the Enlightenment era.

The first feature of conjectural histories that I discussed in the previous section is that they focus on the prehistorical existence of human beings, which lies too far in the past for us to have any materials documenting this kind of life. In other words, conjectural histories trace the origins of society back to a time before the existence of any documents. Relatedly, they focus on the construction of plausible, albeit empirically unproven, conjectures and hypotheses about events in the far past – this is necessary due to lack of available documents that would tell us how prehistory unfolded.

Kant explicitly describes the story he presents in "Conjectural Beginning" as the "presentation of the first history of human beings"[152] and, elsewhere, talks about it in terms of the "first beginning" of the "history of human actions."[153] In addition to focusing on the prehistorical – initial – existence of human beings, he is also comfortable with a broad use of conjectures and hypotheses, of which his account of the beginning of humanity is fully composed. Like for other conjectural historians, for Kant the use of conjectures is tightly linked up with the need to make the transitions in the life of the human being comprehensible: "In the *progression* of history it is indeed allowed to *insert* conjectures in order to fill up gaps in the records, because what precedes as a remote cause and what follows as an effect can provide a quite secure guidance for the discovery of the intermediate causes, so as to make the transition comprehensible."[154] Thus for Kant, as for other writers in this genre, positing hypothetical, plausible scenarios and events in the life of the prehistorical human being can render the present more understandable to us and may shed light on the ways in which the present was shaped through gradual transition in the social life of our species.

---

[152] CB, 8: 115.   [153] CB, 8: 109.   [154] CB, 8: 109.

Kant is also careful to distinguish this enterprise from fact-based historiography by contrasting these two methods of inquiry:

> Nevertheless, since conjectures must not make too high claims on assent, but must always announce themselves as at most only a movement of the power of imagination, accompanying reason and indulged in for the health and recreation of the mind, but not for a serious business, they also cannot compare themselves with that kind of history which is proposed and believed as an actual record about the same occurrence.[155]

Here we may see the suitability of these aspects of conjectural histories for Kant's aim in his "Conjectural Beginning" essay by noting his purpose in this text. As Kant explicitly admits, his aim is not to reconstruct the distant past – this would be empirically impossible given the limitations of our knowledge of prehistorical events. Neither does he want to sketch an entirely fictional and implausible story, which would be useless for his anthropological and ethical purposes.[156] Rather, the story in "Conjectural Beginning" is to be thought of as a possible way in which our species' rational capacities might have emerged that, regardless of whether it is historically accurate, sheds light on the nature of these capacities and their ideal future development.

The feature of conjectural histories that serves Kant well for his purposes, then, is that stories presented through this genre do not purport to be fully accurate historically; rather, their *cognitive* and *explanatory* value consists in presenting a plausible and simplified account of the distant past. This unique way of contributing to the body of knowledge regarding human nature is useful for Kant: since this essay is an explicitly conjectural exercise, it makes sense to put aside the question about the exact epistemic status of the story presented in it, and view it instead as merely possible from the theoretical perspective, but useful from the practical perspective.

There is, notably, a tension between the objective to retain at least some factuality and historical accuracy, even at the level of very general or simplified explanation, and the aim to convey normative prescriptions for our present and future life. On the one hand, conjectural historians, including Kant, draw on scientific data available to them in order not to present a completely fictional account of the past; Herder goes as far so as to claim that the biblical book of Genesis contains a literal, historical account of the distant past. But on the other hand, historical accuracy does not seem to matter if the purpose is to provide guidelines for how to form and maintain a social life. Rousseau even famously writes in the second *Discourse*, a paradigmatic example of a conjectural history, "Let us begin ... by laying facts aside, as they do not affect the question."

---

[155] CB, 8: 109.   [156] CB, 8: 109; see also IUH, 8: 29.

Kant's use of the biblical book of Genesis further supports his (and certain other conjectural history authors') relative lack of interest in factuality, given that Kant does not treat the Bible as a literal source of prehistorical events.

This tension is something that Kant and other conjectural historians, unfortunately, do not address and perhaps do not even see. But is realizing that it is there fatal? One way of making philosophical sense of conjectural histories, and Kant's essay in particular, is to put this tension aside and recognize that the primary role of this essay is to be a guide for an ideal political and moral development of societies and individuals. The role of the speculative history of humanity, then, is subordinate to the former role: namely, to inform these prescriptions, not describe the past. Within this interpretative framework, the question of the factual accuracy of the story is not relevant and the story can be treated as merely hypothetical, not plausible or true.

Like many other conjectural histories, "Conjectural Beginning" also assumes that a specific event in time began human history, postulates specific circumstances of humans' exit from the state of nature, and provides – to an extent – an explanation of the reasons for this exit. As for the circumstances, Kant does not begin with a completely wild animal or, in his words, "with the completely crude state of its nature"; doing so would require too many lengthy and uninteresting conjectures.[157] Rather, he posits a skilled "first human being" who could "*stand* and *walk*," and "speak according to connected words and concepts, hence *think*."[158] He also assumes, following the biblical book of Genesis, that the first human beings were a single couple, living in a garden "richly provisioned by nature with all means of nourishment" and "secured against the attack of predators."[159] (I will return to his extensive use of Genesis later in this section.)

This couple's activities were entirely controlled by an animalistic instinct, a "call of nature," or "that *voice of God* which all animals obey."[160] This instinct provided them with a satisfactory existence without any present or future-oriented worries, and allowed them "a few things for nourishment, but forbade others."[161] But at some point – at a point which Kant does not specify or further characterize, unfortunately – their natural instinct was challenged by a newly awoken faculty of reason, which gave the human being (Kant uses the pronoun 'he' here) an opportunity to compare what his instinct allowed him to eat with that which it did not allow, thus "extend[ing] his knowledge of the means of nourishment beyond the limits of instinct."[162] Reason created within him a desire that was contrary to his natural drives and made him desert

---

[157] CB, 8: 110.   [158] CB, 8: 110.   [159] CB, 8: 110.   [160] CB, 8: 111.   [161] CB, 8: 111.
[162] CB, 8: 111.

his instinct, simultaneously making him "conscious of one's reason as a faculty that can extend itself beyond the limits within which all animals are held."[163] Consequently, he made a choice to eat a fruit which instinct forbade.

This was, according to Kant, the event that began all of human history. But he casts this event in four tightly linked stages, only the first of which was the just-described realization that the human being can choose and act contrary to nature. What followed this radical change in the human's instinct of nourishment was a change in his sexual instinct. He realized that his and his partner's sexual instinct can be modified too – in particular, it can be prolonged and increased through the power of imagination. By withdrawing from the senses that which is desired by another human being (with the use of a fig leaf), he could control and manipulate the other to his own advantage. This was the beginning of inequality between human beings: "*propriety*, an inclination by good conduct to influence others to respect for us (through the concealment of that which could incite low esteem)" was "a genuine foundation of all true sociability."[164]

Reason's third step in emancipating the human being from the kingdom of nature consisted in ceasing to enjoy the present moment due to forming expectations and anxieties about the future: "The man, who had to nourish himself and his spouse, together with the future children, foresaw the ever-growing troubles of his labor."[165] They began to worry about future life and about death, and their only consoling thought was a possible alleviation of hardship for the future generations.

Reason's fourth and last step consisted in their realizing that they, as human beings, are elevated above the other living creatures and can treat them as means to satisfying their own ends. Simultaneously, they comprehended in an obscure manner that they cannot treat other human beings in this way, but must allow them equality:

> The first time he [the new human] said to the sheep: Nature has given you the skin you wear not for you but for me, then took it off the sheep and put it on himself (Genesis 3:21), he became aware of a prerogative that he had by his nature over all animals . . . . *This representation includes (however obscurely) the thought of the opposite: that he must not say something like this to any human being, but has to regard him as an equal participant in the gifts of nature – a preparation from afar for the restrictions that reason was to lay on the will in the future in regard to his fellow human beings,* and which far more than inclination and love is necessary to the establishment of society. *And thus the human being had entered into an equality with all rational beings,* of

---

[163] CB, 8: 112.   [164] CB, 8: 113.   [165] CB, 8: 113.

whatever rank they might be (Genesis 3:22); namely, in regard to the claim of being himself an end, of also being esteemed as such by everyone else, and *of being used by no one merely as a means to other ends.*[166]

The four steps reason took in elevating the human being above nature may be seen as a delineation of several stages characterizing human development – a feature typical for conjectural histories. However, later in the text Kant uses a more standard way of categorizing early human development according to distinct stages – more reminiscent of Smith's undertaking in the *Wealth of Nations.* In the "Close of the Story" section of "Conjectural Beginning," Kant depicts a later time in humanity's development and returns to discussing it in terms of entire societies, not a single biblical couple. The first phase was one of growing labor and discord – "the prelude to the unification of society" – during which humans possessed crops and domesticated animals, first leading "the savage life of hunters," then living "the pastoral life,"[167] which was more secure than the previous stage. Growing conflicts with others drew the human being to distance himself from them, which began the third epoch of agriculture. This, in turn, led to the creation of villages and, with it, the beginning of culture and art, of civil constitution, public justice, and government. Here Kant also mentions the growing dangers of war and hostility between different settlements.

Like Ferguson, Rousseau, and Hume, Kant exhibits an ambivalent attitude toward progress throughout the "Conjectural Beginning." This is evident both in his description of the human being's initial emancipation from nature and in his depiction of the gradual development of human history later on. For Kant, human progress is an important feature of his essay and his philosophy of history at large, but this progress is neither inevitable nor linear. When he portrays the first step of reason's awakening, he directly follows it up with a remark that it brough with it fear, anxiety, and uncertainty: "Yet upon momentary delight that this marked superiority [over other species] might have awakened in him, anxiety and fright must have followed right away, concerning how he, who still did not know the hidden properties and remote effects of any thing, should deal with this newly discovered faculty."[168] Reason's third step – the expectation of the future – also brought with it similar emotions: it is an "inexhaustible source of cares and worries which the uncertain future incites and from which all animals are exempt."[169] Reason's awakening, therefore, immediately brought with it a departure from a blissful existence of satisfaction – from paradise – and the struggles of facing an unknown and untrodden path of the development of human capacities. Kant sums it up

---

[166] CB, 8: 114, emphasis added.   [167] CB, 8: 118.   [168] CB, 8: 112.   [169] CB, 8: 113.

himself in the following way: "The first step out of this condition [nature], therefore was on the moral side a *fall*; on the physical side, a multitude of ills of life hitherto unknown were the consequence of this fall."[170]

In "Close of the Story," Kant's portrait of humankind's subsequent transitions from the hunter and gatherer society to a civilized state also features a multitude of remarks aimed at challenging a simple vision of humanity's linear progress. Every transition – from the hunter and gatherer to pastoral life, from pastoral life to agriculture, and from agriculture to the civilized state – is marked by conflict, hostility, and the drive to live a peaceful life. Kant sees war both as an ill that oppresses humankind and as a force necessary for its further development. Moreover, he warns us not to attribute our misery to providence or to the ancestral sin from Genesis, but to take full responsibility for it and for the betterment of the human race: his story is supposed to show the human being

> that he must not blame providence for the ills that oppress him; that he is also not justified in ascribing his own misdeeds to an original crime of his ancestral parents, ... but rather that he must recognize with full right what they did as having done by himself and attribute the responsibility for all ills arising from the misuse of his reason entirely to himself.[171]

I have so far shown how the "Conjectural Beginning" essay fits with some of the features characteristic of conjectural histories. I will now argue that Kant's essay differs from the paradigmatic conjectural histories of the time in important ways. In particular, I will make the following two points. First, Kant does not follow the trend of abandoning the framework of Genesis and any notion of divine providence. Rather, he draws heavily on the notion of divine Christian providence, and hence recourses to a non-naturalistic explanation of human progress. Second, Kant does not follow other conjectural historians in casting the developmental story of humankind in terms of the original sources that prompt it rather than in a teleological way. Instead, he draws heavily on teleological notions of human progress and perfectionism that are characteristic of his philosophy of history at large.

Going back to the first point, Kant does not firmly step away from a religious account of human and social development, like most conjectural histories, but rather claims to "make use of a holy document [the Book of Genesis] as my map."[172] For example, he positions the first, primitive humans of his story in the Garden of Eden, equates the first free choice they made with eating fruit from the forbidden tree, and regards animal instinct as synonymous with the voice of God.[173] His entire account of reason's awakening and humankind's emancipation

---

[170] CB, 8: 115.   [171] CB, 8: 122.   [172] CB, 8: 109.   [173] CB, 8: 110–12.

from the forces of nature is a reinterpretation and rewriting of the biblical story of the Garden of Eden and Adam and Eve's exile from Paradise. The first step of reason's awakening is equated with the human being's choice to eat a fruit from the tree forbidden by natural instinct, and hence by the voice of God. However, in Kant's version of the story it is not the snake (satan) who tempts the human to go against God; rather, it is reason itself. Kant also calls the decision to eat the wrong fruit a "fall," thus evoking the idea of the original sin and the misery that followed. The second step of reason's awakening, in turn, evokes the biblical story of the sexual shame Adam and Eve felt for the first time after their exile from Paradise, and their subsequent decision to cover themselves with the fig leaf.

More surprisingly, Kant continues to insert biblical references into his essay long after he is done with presenting the story of reason's initial awakening. In the later part of his text, where he is concerned with analyzing what reason's awakening meant for humankind and with sketching further stages of human history, he makes consistent references to Genesis.

Not only does Kant make an extensive use of Genesis, but he also draws heavily on the notion of divine Christian providence, and hence recourses to a non-naturalistic explanation of human progress.[174] This is especially evident in the "Concluding Remark" of his essay, which Kant begins by claiming that humans have a tendency to ascribe their misery and worries as the work (or fault) of providence: "The thinking human being feels a sorrow, one which can even become a moral corruption, of which the thoughtless knows nothing: namely, discontent with the providence that governs the course of the world on the whole, when he estimates the ills that so much oppress humankind, and (as it appears) leaves it with no hope for anything better."[175] Kant does not entirely criticize this tendency to provide providential explanations for certain events, but rather goes on to explain that such explanations cannot be taken as the only source of the world's ills: "it is of the greatest importance to be content with providence . . . , partly in order to grasp courage even among our toils, and partly so that by placing responsibility for it on fate, we might not lose sight of our own responsibility, which perhaps might be the sole cause of all these ills, and avoid the remedy against them, which consists in self-improvement."[176] It is therefore only by assuming responsibility for all the hardships that we have faced that we can improve our nature and the course of human history – and make progress. Kant echoes this point at the very end of his essay by emphasizing that the story of reason's emergence – and, in particular, the human being's

---

[174] See, for example, CB, 8: 121, 8: 123.   [175] CB, 8: 120–21.   [176] CB, 8: 121.

own decision to make the first use of reason – must show us that we are the key actors in humankind's progress:

> Such a presentation of his history is beneficial and serviceable to the human being for his instruction and improvement by showing him that he must not blame providence for the ills that oppress him . . . . And thus the result of an oldest history of humanity attempted by philosophy is contentment with providence and with the course of things human on the whole.[177]

To be sure, Kant not only alters the story presented in Genesis for his own purposes rather than faithfully following it, but his use of the Bible does not mean he believes that the events presented there literally took place in the far past. This is evident in Kant's own criticism of Herder's literal understanding of the Bible in the *Oldest Document of Mankind*, which Kant critiques in his review of this work. Kant also implicitly criticizes Herder's treatment of Genesis by being explicit in "Conjectural Beginning" that a historiography based on the Bible is only of conjectural and speculative value.[178] As Wood writes, "Kant was especially contemptuous of Herder's ... apparent belief that ... the accounts of the Garden of Eden and the fall can be regarded, on the basis of comparison with other ancient histories, as a reliable historical account of the beginnings of the human species."[179] This departure from Herder is evident in the opening statement to "Conjectural Beginning" ("since conjectures must not make too high claims on assent, but must always announce themselves as at most only a movement of the power of imagination, accompanying reason and indulged in for the recreation and health of the mind"[180]), in Kant's broad re-interpretation of the biblical story of choosing to eat a fruit from the tree of knowledge, and in his "Concluding Remark" to the essay, where he instructs us how the preceding anthropological account should be read.

Nonetheless, even his more serious and large-scale account of the agricultural and technical development of societies,[181] which follows the conjectural story of reason's emergence and the exit from the state of nature, draws heavily on Genesis. The essay in its entirety can hardly be described as a departure from a biblical explanation of human development.

Another distinct feature of Kant's essay is his use of teleology and the related introduction of an account of the development of moral – as opposed to merely social and political – capacities and ways of reasoning in the human being. The strongest pronouncement of Kant's teleology is perhaps evident when he writes that human history "does not start from good and progress toward evil, but develops gradually from the worse toward the better; and each of us, for his part,

---

[177] CB, 8: 123.   [178] Beiser 1987, 149–52.   [179] Wood 2007, 160.   [180] CB, 8: 109.
[181] CB, 8: 115–120.

is called upon by nature itself to contribute as much as lies in his power to this progress."[182] The first use of reason is portrayed by Kant as the end of the human being's life in the deterministic state of nature, where he was governed entirely by heteronomous forces, and the beginning of the challenging pathway from realizing one is free to learning to control this freedom with appropriate sociopolitical and moral conduct. One element of Kant's teleological treatment of this lengthy path is his emphasis on the impossibility to return back the "dominion of instinct" once the capacity for reasoning had been exercised: "from this estate of freedom," Kant writes, "once he tasted it, it was nevertheless wholly impossible for him to turn back again to that of servitude (under the dominion of instinct)."[183]

Another element of Kant's teleological treatment of human history is evident in the fourth step of reason's awakening, when he casts the first human being's realization that he must treat other members of his species as equal to him in terms of "a preparation from afar for the restrictions that reason was to lay on the will in the future in regard to his fellow human beings."[184] This passage clearly demonstrates reason's directedness in shaping the human will to conform ever more to the requirements of morality, which bind it. It also implies that the process of learning how to conduct oneself in a moral way, and understanding why one ought to do so, will be a lengthy process and one that requires appropriate societal arrangements that are not yet in place. The latter aspect of learning to conduct oneself in a moral way is also evident when Kant writes, shortly after, that "culture must proceed in order properly to develop the predispositions of humanity as a moral species to their vocation, so that the latter no longer conflict with humanity as a natural species."[185]

Finally, a teleological treatment of this topic by Kant is also displayed in his justification of the suffering that reason's first use brought onto our species. Conflicts, wars, worries about the future, and anxiety are all indispensable, "natural" elements of human progress and, as such, play a role in the purposive plan that leads to the moralization of humanity. While, on the one hand, we must see ourselves as responsible for our mistakes and for learning how to properly use reason, we may also regard the large-scale view of human history as arranged purposively: "The individual therefore has cause to ascribe all ills he suffers, and all the evil he perpetrates, to his own guilt, yet at the same time as a member of the whole (of a species), also to admire and to praise the wisdom and purposiveness of the arrangement."[186] This thought is echoed in Kant's later remark that "all true ills that oppress human life . . . are in themselves good and purposive as natural predispositions."[187]

---

[182] CB, 8: 123.   [183] CB, 8: 112.   [184] CB, 8: 114.   [185] CB, 8: 116.   [186] CB, 8: 116.
[187] CB, 8: 117–18.

Kant's "Conjectural Beginning" essay fits with many of the features characteristic of conjectural histories: focus on the prehistorical existence of human beings before the existence of any documents; drawing conjectures and hypotheses about events in the far past rather than relying on facts; assuming that a specific event in time began human history; postulating the circumstances of humans' exit from the state of nature; assuming that conflict and warfare are indispensable for human development; and exhibiting an ambivalent attitude toward human progress. However, Kant also expands and challenges the boundaries of this genre in a number of ways. He makes use of the biblical book of Genesis in a very extensive way (albeit does not treat it literally) and relies on a divine, providential account of humankind's emergence from the state of nature. His account of human history and its progress is also teleological and involves an account of the development of moral – as opposed to merely social and political – capacities and ways of reasoning in the human being.

3 Pluralistic Thinking and Reason's Future Development

3.1 Introduction

As we have seen in the previous two sections of this Element, Kant offers a conjectural account of the way our species have been gradually learning to make a mature or enlightened use of practical reason in his essays "Universal History with a Cosmopolitan Aim" and "Conjectural Beginning of Human History" from the 1780s. Such mature use of reason, as he explains a few years later in the published version of his anthropology lectures, is characterized by abandoning the standpoint of "practical egoism," which amounts to giving deliberative weight only to one's own happiness,[188] and learning how to exercise the psychological disposition to "pluralism": endorsing "the way of thinking in which one is not concerned with oneself as the whole world, but rather regards and conducts oneself as a mere citizen of the world."[189] According to this view, the pluralist possesses the ability to empathize with others, consider their needs during deliberation, and participate in judgments that are universally valid. This ability is grounded in the pluralist's self-conception as a citizen of the world, recognizing themselves as a member of the community of all human beings who are equally subject to universal law.[190]

Kant is never explicit about what is required in order to become a pluralist, nor does he explain what it means to be a pluralist beyond the brief remark

---

[188] Anth, 7: 130.   [189] Anth, 7: 130.
[190] Kant's conception of pluralism, on which I will shortly elaborate, differs in significant ways from contemporary usages of this term, largely grounded in Rawls's late philosophical work

in*Anthropology* (cited earlier). This part of my Element takes a detailed look at this under-studied notion of pluralism and explicates the features of pluralistic thinking. My aim here is to offer a novel account of Kant's pluralism and to connect it to the notions of public use of reason, the three maxims of common human understanding, and the role played by interpersonal communication in advancing the progress of our rational capacities.

The shift to the concept of pluralism in this part of the Element is motivated by its importance for Kant's philosophy of history, which I have demonstrated in Section 1.3. As I have argued at length there, the progress of the human being and humanity as a whole can be described as consisting in eliminating within oneself the standpoint of a practical egoist and striving to adopt the opposite standpoint – as Kant puts it in *Anthropology*, the standpoint of a "pluralist." Indeed, Kant explicitly contrasts egoism with pluralism: "The opposite of egoism can only be pluralism, that is, the way of thinking in which one is not concerned with oneself as the whole world, but rather regards and conducts oneself as a mere citizen of the world [*Weltbürger*]."[191] Furthermore, the concept of pluralism, the definition of which includes the term "citizen of the world [*Weltbürger*]," is also directly linked to Kant's teleological conception of the progress of human history, since its cognate is used to define the ideal

---

(Rawls 1993). In contemporary political philosophy, pluralism is a non-normative term that refers to the factual existence of multiple (often irreconcilable) philosophical, scientific, moral, socioeconomic, and religious worldviews among citizens of the same nation – a fact that poses a challenge when it comes to settling on laws, policies, and norms acceptable to all citizens. Rawls's conception of "reasonable pluralism" is a narrower normative notion, according to which a well-ordered (liberal) society ought to consist of a plurality of reasonable comprehensive doctrines whose political elements overlap in such a way that agreement on political matters is possible despite the differing philosophical, moral, and religious commitments of its citizens. Kant's conception of pluralism denotes, by contrast, a psychological disposition that each and every person should develop – a disposition that is not only political, but also moral in its character. As I will show in the next section, the Kantian pluralistic perspective of reason involves thinking independently by following the maxim "think for oneself," thinking from others' perspectives by following the maxim "think from the standpoint of others," and maintaining consistency of thought by following the maxim "think consistently." These maxims (and in particular the first two) guide one to assume one's coexistence in a community with other moral beings and to regard oneself as governed by the universal law which governs the pursuit of everyone's conceptions of happiness. However, the Rawlsian conception of reasonability which every liberal citizen's comprehensive doctrine ought to express arguably comes close to the Kantian conception of pluralism of reason. Indeed, some commentators (especially Forst 2017) have argued – against Rawls's explicit separation of the moral (which is private) from the political (which is public) in his later work – that his theory of socio-political justice for a liberal society, the core of which is his conception of reasonable pluralism, is Kantian because it is autonomous and morally grounded: "It is autonomous in that it is based on practical reason as the capacity of autonomous citizens who respect each other as free and equal to reciprocally and generally justify and accept principles of justice. And it is moral insofar as it has an independent normative force that is strong enough to outweigh other, competing values" (Forst 2017, 143).
[191] Anth, 7: 130.

"cosmopolitan [*weltbürgerlicher*] condition" between states in "Universal History."[192] As I have shown in Section 1.3.2, the progress of our species at large, and in particular the right treatment of others within a large community – the *telos* of humankind's progress – has to be achieved via two separate, but mutually reinforcing, processes: one internal (arriving at the disposition to pluralism within every human being) and one external (arriving at the political condition of cosmopolitanism).

The section is divided into two main subsections. Section 3.2 aims to advance a deeper understanding of what it means to be a pluralist, and to look specifically at the distinct characteristics of the pluralistic perspective of reason. The central question addressed in this subsection is: How can one be a pluralist in the correct manner? I show that being a pluralist necessitates adhering to the following conditions: thinking independently by following the maxim "think for oneself," utilizing public reason or thinking from others' perspectives by following the maxim "think from the standpoint of others," and maintaining consistency of thought by following the maxim "think consistently." Section 3.3 highlights Kant's interest in the development or enlightenment of reason both in individual human beings and the human race as a whole. Here I draw primarily from *Lectures on Pedagogy* to examine the connection between an individual's maturation and the advancement of humankind.

3.2 The Norms of Pluralistic Thinking

As we have already seen, according to Kant's "Conjectural Beginning," the first humans who started using reason had a tendency toward practical egoism: giving deliberative weight only to one's own happiness. This led to the emergence of an unjust juridical order motivated by individual self-interest and competitiveness. However, the gradual improvement of our juridical order appears to be associated with a psychological disposition that opposes practical egoism: the disposition to pluralism. Kant argues in his essays from the 1780s and in his published *Anthropology* that for a truly just juridical order to exist, its members must be pluralists in his sense of this word. This means assuming and accepting coexistence in a community with others (as world citizens) and regarding oneself as governed by the universal law that regulates the pursuit of different conceptions of happiness.

Kant's pluralism is not solely a political concept, but primarily an ethical one. It refers not only to a particular way of acting in response to heteronomous incentives, but also to a specific way of structuring one's motivational psychology. In his definition of pluralism in *Anthropology*, Kant uses the normative

---

[192] IUH, 8: 25–26.

terms "community" and "world." Being part of a global community of human beings has significant practical implications for one's actions. For example, it restricts the permissible actions that further one's happiness, given their potential impact on other members of the community. The underlying idea is that all rational community members have an equal claim to freedom, which justifies such restrictions.[193]

Furthermore, Kantian pluralism depicts not only a concern for other people's desires and goals which may differ from mine (a position commonly referred to as 'altruism'), but also an understanding that, since people have different conceptions of happiness and their preferences are contingent, pursuing happiness as such cannot be a universal law. Hence pluralism encompasses not only altruism, but also a regard for oneself as governed by the universally valid moral principle that regulates the pursuit of everybody's happiness. To be a pluralist means not only to be able to see things from other people's perspectives, but also actually to interact with those unlike oneself in order collectively to settle on ways of discharging the duties that stem from the requirements of morality, which bind all of us. Importantly, it does not suffice to conduct oneself in a way that takes into account the potential impact one's actions could have on other members of the community; the pluralist must also *believe* that other members of the world-wide human community to which he belongs have an equal claim to freedom, and hence that their happiness needs to be given deliberative weight.

I am now going to consider what is required in order to be a pluralist – to reflect on the normative features or components of the pluralistic standpoint of reason. To do so, I will present what I take to be the necessary conditions of being a pluralist[194]:

(1) abiding by the maxim "think for oneself" (thinking freely);
(2) abiding by the maxim "think from the standpoint of others" (making public use of one's reason);
(3) abiding by the maxim "think consistently."

While these three maxims of common human understanding have been widely discussed in Kant scholarship, no attempts have been made to conceptually connect them with Kant's conception of pluralism and the related idea of

---

[193] Despite the fact that Kant's pluralism is an ethical as well as a political notion, it bears close resemblance to Rousseau's social contract – a strictly political notion. Arguably, Kant intended his kingdom of ends (comprised of pluralistically minded members) to be an ethical counterpart of Rousseau's social contract.

[194] By "being a pluralist," I mean actually making use of the disposition to pluralism, not just being disposed to do so.

a pluralistic standpoint of reason from his *Anthropology*.[195] The remainder of section will show how Kant's pluralism and his three maxims of common human understanding relate to one another.

3.2.1 "Think For Oneself"

Kant considers the ability to think freely as a crucial requirement for being a pluralist. In Kant's view, thinking freely is equivalent to adhering to the first maxim of common human understanding, which is "think for oneself."[196] Kant describes this maxim in most detail in his "Enlightenment" and "Orientation" essays as well as in several other texts.[197]

This first maxim is arguably the most foundational maxim enabling rational autonomy. A person who thinks freely or thinks for herself is able critically to reflect on her beliefs and desires instead of blindly following the prescriptions of others. The maxim "think for oneself" or the requirement to think freely is described in the "Enlightenment," "Orientation," the third *Critique*, and *Anthropology* as a negative principle: one must not rely (unquestioningly) on the authoritative claims of others – a kind of behavior that characterizes private uses of reason[198] – but rather on the authority of one's *own* rational and critical capacities. In third *Critique*, Kant describes this maxim as "the maxim of the *unprejudiced* way of thinking"[199] adopted by people who do not rely on the opinions of others (heteronomy of reason). Adopting this maxim therefore requires that we think of ourselves as deliberative agents capable of making sound judgments independently of others.[200] As Deligiorgi puts it, "The change from submission to external authority to submission to the authority of one's own reason is a condition for undertaking what is required to make good this claim to authority, namely, the commitment to autonomous reasoning."[201] Only then, O'Neill suggests, will we be able to hear and debate a plurality of viewpoints expressed by people whose thinking is independent.[202]

The ability to think independently or freely is closely linked to the second requirement of being a pluralist – thinking from the standpoint of others or using public reason. This refers to the appropriate method of structuring our rational deliberation and communication with others. However, the condition of free thinking, or thinking for oneself, emphasizes the importance of arriving at the

---

[195] See, for example, O'Neill 1989, 1992; Velkley 1989; Neiman 1994; Weinstock 1996; Munzel 1999; Deligiorgi 2002, 2005; Patrone 2008.

[196] Free thinking is discussed by Kant in the "Enlightenment" and "Orientation" essays. The three maxims of common human understanding appear in slightly different formulations in three places: CJ, 5: 294–95, Anth, 7: 200, JL, 9: 57.

[197] See also CJ, 5: 294–95, Anth, 7: 200, JL, 9: 57.   [198] See WIE, 8: 37.   [199] CJ, 5: 294.

[200] See WIE, 8: 35, WOT, 8: 146f, Anth, 7: 228–29.   [201] Deligiorgi 2005, 93.

[202] O'Neill 1989, 46.

decision to reason in a public way *on our own*, rather than being coerced or convinced by someone else. Therefore, our motivation to reason publicly and communicate with others in an appropriate manner must arise from an autonomous process of deliberation, or free thinking, that is not influenced by external intellectual constraints. As Kant writes in *Anthropology*, as a child, I "let others think for [me] and merely imitated others or allowed them to guide [me] by leading-strings."[203] However, at some point I must exit this immaturity and adopt the maxim of thinking for myself. If an adult chooses to remain in a state of immaturity even when she possesses the ability to overcome it, it is considered "self-incurred"[204] and blameworthy; this state of affairs differs from the natural and unavoidable immaturity of a child.

But Kant stresses that the process of exiting immaturity also has a social and cooperative aspect, as it can only occur in a social setting. While other people may influence an individual's decision to endorse the maxim of thinking for oneself and provide opportunities for developing reasoning skills and motivations, it is ultimately up to the individual to make the autonomous decision to use these opportunities and cultivate these skills and motivations. Therefore, leaving behind immaturity is a crucial first-personal decision in an individual's life, and the first step toward enlightenment – or, as Kant writes in *Anthropology*, "the most important revolution from within the human being."[205]

The ability to use autonomous reasoning is a fundamental aspect of our humanity that we develop throughout our lives. It entails making our own reasoning the source of the rules and principles that direct our thoughts and behaviors. This responsibility is linked to the fact that we possess positive freedom, which means that our will is structured in a way that compels us to adopt principles of action that are acceptable to all rational beings. Our freedom is not merely negative (i.e., the ability to act independently of external causes like the laws of nature) but also positive, in that we are motivated to act on universally acceptable maxims.[206] (This is what Kant calls in the *Groundwork* "the will's property of being a law to itself."[207])

Kant discusses the potential for autonomous thinking and the attainment of enlightenment also in his "Orientation" essay. There, he posits that this is linked to the ability to communicate freely with others, asserting that maintaining the freedom to engage with rational individuals is essential for preserving our capability to think autonomously: "the same external constraint that deprives people of the freedom to communicate their thoughts in public also removes

---

[203] Anth, 7: 229.   [204] WIE, 8: 41, Anth, 7: 229.   [205] Anth, 7: 229.   [206] G, 4: 446–49.
[207] G, 4: 447.

their freedom of thought."[208] Similarly, in "Theory and Practice" he connects freedom of expression with the public use of reason:

> a citizen must have, with the approval of the ruler himself, the authorization to make known publicly his opinions about what it is in the ruler's arrangements that seems to him to be a wrong against the commonwealth. For, to assume that the head of state could never err or be ignorant of something would be to represent him as favored with divine inspiration and raised above humanity. Thus *freedom of the pen* (. . .) is the sole palladium of the people's rights.[209]

Freedom of expression, Kant claims here, is important during any communication with the sovereign and for improving any issues within a commonwealth. The final sentence of the cited passage can also be interpreted as a warning that freedom of expression does not equate to the freedom to engage in any behavior or join any (political) movement – the liberty to deliberate on reasons does not imply the freedom to act on those reasons.

Chronologically speaking, "Orientation" is the first place (1786) where Kant presents all three maxims of common human understanding as a coherent set of maxims. Prior to 1786, there is no mention of the three maxims as such. Of course, in "What is Enlightenment?" (published two years earlier) Kant talks about a principle that he will later label the first maxim, calling it "the propensity or calling to think freely"[210] or "the calling of each individual to think for himself."[211] But this principle is discussed in isolation from the other two and it is not explicitly called a maxim. On these grounds, one may suspect that Kant did not come to terms with the three maxims of common human understanding until 1786, even though they (especially the first one) were implicitly in the background of his theorizing about rational development and interpersonal communication.

3.2.2 "Think from the Standpoint of Others"

In the "Orientation," Kant concludes that the standard for following the first maxim "think for oneself" is to reason based on principles that could be considered valid for all rational beings: "*Thinking for oneself* means . . . no more than to ask oneself, whenever one is supposed to assume something, whether one could find it feasible to make the ground or the rule on which one assumes it into a universal principle for the use of reason."[212] This formulation of the first maxim shows how it leads to the second one: "think from the standpoint of others." As formulated in *Critique of Judgment*, the second maxim

---

[208] WOT, 8: 144.   [209] TP, 8: 304; original emphasis.   [210] WIE, 8: 41.   [211] WIE, 8: 36.
[212] WOT, 8: 146n.

consists in one's capacity to "set [one]self apart from the subjective private conditions of the judgement, within which so many others are as if bracketed, and [to] reflect on his own judgement from a *universal standpoint* (which he can only determined by putting himself into the standpoint of others)."[213] This maxim of liberal, enlarged, or broad-minded thinking[214] emphasizes the difficulty of using one's reason properly after becoming accustomed to relying solely on one's own reasoning instead of that of others. The second essential condition for being a pluralist is thus adhering to this maxim: a person is a pluralist if she thinks from the standpoint of others.

The maxim of thinking from the standpoint of others or of making public use of one's reason governs the following aspects of being a pluralist: (i) thinking as though one was about to address the entire "society of citizens in the world,"[215] (ii) actually addressing the world at large, and (iii) in so doing regarding oneself as a member of the community of all human beings. To show why this is the case, I will draw primarily on Kant's discussion of the function of making public use of reason from the "Enlightenment" essay. In this essay, Kant defines the public use of one's reason in the following way:

> The public use of one's reason must always be free . . . . [B]y the public use of one's own reason I understand that use which someone makes of it as a scholar before the entire public of the world of readers ... insofar as ... [one] regards [one]self as a member of a whole commonwealth, even of the society of citizens in the world.[216]

This definition of the public use of reason presupposes the intellectual autonomy of the individual who makes the public use of her *own* reason, which is already established by the first maxim. The ability to critically reflect on one's beliefs and desires is a prerequisite for making public use of reason. Blindly following intellectual, political, or religious authorities (referred to as "guardians" by Kant) is thus incompatible with making public use of reason.

Kant's definition of the public use of reason suggests that to make such a use of reason means to address the entire world at large ("the society of citizens in the world," "a whole commonwealth") instead of specific people. As O'Neill makes clear, "[t]he notion of a *public* use of reason is ... defined in terms of the *audience* whom an act of communication may reach."[217] For example, public intellectuals aiming at influencing the public opinion by expressing themselves in popular media should exercise reason in a public way. (Kant himself wrote numerous pieces of this kind, including his *Essays regarding the Philantropinum*.) This means that Kant poses certain constraints on the way

---

[213] CJ Section 40, 5: 295.   [214] See Anth, 7: 228, CJ, 5: 294.   [215] WIE, 8: 37.
[216] WIE, 8: 37.   [217] O'Neill 1989, 32.

one can communicate to the entire community of human beings: one should only say things that could be understood by (rendered intelligible to) the world community. The pursuit of an unrestricted audience is meaningful only if we can communicate in ways that are generally understandable. A real debate requires mutual comprehension, rather than hostile speaking past one another or dependence on some external authority.

It is worth noting that Kant's distinction between the public and private spheres of reasoning does not align with modern usage of these terms. Typically, the private sphere denotes thought that is unconstrained by external factors, while the public sphere may be governed by law. However, for Kant, individuals in public positions must only use reason in a private sense, meaning their reasoning is limited by an authority outside of reason itself, and therefore not grounded in universal principles of reason. In contrast, public use of reason involves being free from non-universal principles imposed by an external authority and being free from lawlessness and arbitrariness.[218] To use reason publicly means to focus on the formal and necessary features of human rationality rather than on one's specific situation in the world, and considering possible judgments others could make rather than their actual contingent judgments. Public reason is only constrained by its own autonomous principles that are shareable among all humans and fundamental to human reasoning.[219] These principles are not guided by a local authority, as there is no external authority accepted by all rational thinkers.

The requirement to address the entire world at large is thus the requirement to structure our reflection in a way that takes into account whether our reasons can be considered as universally valid. This requirement connects the public use of reason with the ethical requirement to treat all human beings as autonomous rational agents with equal claims to freedom. In the "Orientation" essay Kant redescribes this aspect of making public use of reason in a way that suggests a 'universalizability' criterion:

> To make use of one's own reason [in a public way] means no more than to ask oneself, whenever one is supposed to assume something, whether one could find it feasible to make the ground or the rule on which one assumes it into a universal principle for the use of reason. . . . [W]ith this examination he will see superstition and enthusiasm disappear, even if he falls far short of having the information to refute them on objective grounds.[220]

According to Kant, therefore, engaging in regular public use of reason involves, among other things, arranging our rational deliberation in a manner that could

---

[218] See also Bittner 1974, 194–96; O'Neill 1992, 297–99; Höffe 1997.
[219] See WOT, 8: 145–46, CPR A747/B775.   [220] WOT, 8: 146f.

be comprehended and approved by all rational deliberators. This is what it means to give proper consideration to other rational deliberators.

Furthermore, regularly making public use of reason describes a certain way of thinking as well as a certain way of speaking or communicating. These two are closely related: as Wood puts it, "[t]hinking itself is a *social* activity because it must be critical, testing what is thought from a plurality of standpoints in order to achieve unity."[221] Regularly making public use of reason describes a certain way of thinking because it needs to pass the *hypothetical* test of being understandable and intelligible to the entire world of rational deliberators. But it also pertains to a particular mode of communication, as pluralism demands a specific approach to interacting with others, which sets boundaries for interpersonal communication. This approach assumes that others are also autonomous rational agents who possess the same entitlement to freedom as I do, by virtue of our shared humanity, and thus must be respected accordingly. If a deliberative agent regularly makes public use of her reason and thereby examines whether her beliefs and claims could be accepted by others (considered as universally valid), then she is ready to *actually* (instead of merely hypothetically) engage in the right kind of interpersonal communication. Actually communicating in such a way is crucial to the project of collectively clarifying, and learning about, moral principles that ought to guide us all. This is because exchanging opinions is a necessary step in testing and comparing them, which in turn allows us to arrive at better practical norms as a group. Kant emphasizes repeatedly that our human capacities can only develop and improve in a social context. In *Anthropology*, for example, he writes: "with all other animals left to themselves, each individual reaches its complete destiny [*Bestimmung*]; however with the human being only the species, at best, reaches it."[222]

Kant's understanding of the public use of reason differs from contemporary accounts of public reason and pluralism, such as those put forth by Rawls and Gaus. Kant's notion of public use of reason is not limited to regulating political participation or government decision-making processes. Rather, it refers to the ability to reason in a way that can be comprehended and debated by a community of public intellectuals interested in the topic, regardless of whether their opinions are popular in such a community. This ability to make public use of one's own reason applies to public discussions beyond strictly political matters. Furthermore, it requires both freedom of consciousness and freedom of expression.

For Rawls, Gaus, and other contemporary public reason theorists, pluralism is a problem for democratic theory: that people have different reasonable conceptions of the good and that they face reasonable disagreement about

---

[221] Wood 1999, 302; emphasis original.   [222] Anth, 7: 324. See also IUH, 8: 18–9.

their beliefs are facts about our society, and we need a system that enables all people to engage in political participation despite this pluralism. For Rawls, public reason is a solution to the challenge of pluralism: it is a standard for decision-making in the political sphere and for political legitimacy that is acceptable to all reasonable members of the community.[223] Gaus's conception of justificatory liberalism takes this standard to be the epistemic criterion of reasonability that applies to individual beliefs, not to comprehensive doctrines or sets of beliefs endorsed by reasonable individuals.[224] (As Gaus has argued, even reasonable people often hold some unreasonable beliefs.[225]) Kant's pluralism acknowledges the existence of multiple ideas of happiness and the need to distinguish between morality, which is universally valid, and happiness, which is contingent, to construct a moral universe in which everyone has an equal place. When Kant speaks of making public use of reason, he refers to the ability to express and debate one's opinions in writing, rather than equal political participation or decision-making. His approach is more aligned with Gaus's justificatory liberalism than Rawls's political liberalism because both frameworks encompass a broader range of beliefs than solely political beliefs and focus on how specific opinions are formed rather than an individual's entire set of beliefs.

Furthermore, Kant posits that using reason in a public manner entails recognizing oneself as a member of the community of all human beings when addressing the world as a whole. This aspect of thinking from the standpoint of others and utilizing reason publicly builds on the previous aspect: in order to ensure that my reasoning can be comprehended and embraced by all other human beings, I must also view myself as an active participant in the human community. Shaping my rational deliberation in a public manner necessitates acknowledging myself as a constituent of this community. This element of the public use of reason, just like Kant's notions of cosmopolitanism (from "Universal History") and of pluralism (from *Anthropology*), presupposes the agent's regarding herself a world citizen. In all three definitions – of pluralism (in *Anthropology*), of cosmopolitanism (in "Universal History"), and of public use of reason (in "Enlightenment") – Kant makes use of the same term: "citizen of the world" [*Weltbürger*].

3.2.3 "Think Consistently"

The third necessary condition of being a pluralist is abiding by the maxim "think consistently" or, as Kant terms it in the third *Critique*, "always to think in accord with oneself"[226]: a person is a pluralist if she thinks in a consistent manner. Unlike the preceding two maxims of common human understanding, this

---

[223] Rawls 1993.   [224] Gaus 1999: 273–82.   [225] Gaus 1995.   [226] CJ, 5: 294.

maxim embodies a broader commitment to rationality as a means-end coherence and a manner of thinking that is unified by shared principles, as mandated by reason. In essence, it is a repudiation of arbitrariness and lawlessness.

Deligiorgi has argued that the maxim "think consistently" represents only the need to apply the previous two maxims in a consistent and regular manner: "Consistency is here [in the third maxim] put to the task of joining together the negative moment of intellectual emancipation, the throwing off of the 'yoke of immaturity', with the positive moment of autonomy through which we seek to override the narrowly subjective conditions of our judgement."[227] In a similar vein, G. Felicitas Munzel has interpreted the maxim of consistent thinking as "the union of the first two maxims"[228] and "the consummation of the first two."[229]

In my view, interpreting Kant's third maxim of common human understanding solely as a call for the consistent and regular application of the first two maxims is a mistake. This is because the first two maxims already contain within them the requirement of regular adherence, as they are intended to guide the development of practical rationality and intellectual flourishing through normative principles of good thinking. Additionally, the third maxim should have a unique and separate meaning, rather than simply serving to direct the application of the previous two maxims, given its equal standing with them. The maxim of consistent thinking requires holding noncontradictory beliefs that are unified under reason's common principles. The beliefs one holds have to be not only logically consistent, but also systematic in the sense described in the "Architectonic" of the first *Critique*.[230] Since reason's end is unity under principles,[231] thinking must be consistent if it is to count as the exercise of a skill and if it is to achieve reason's end. Consistent thinking includes being accountable to oneself as a rational autonomous being as well as to others with whom one may enter into a discussion. As the Kingdom of Ends formulation of the Categorical Imperative[232] suggests, being rationally autonomous already involves accountability to one's community.

Deligiorgi and Munzel are therefore incorrect in their understanding of the third maxim, which suggests that it only combines the first two and emphasizes the importance of applying them consistently. Although this interpretation may

---

[227] Deligiorgi 2002, 151.   [228] Munzel 1999, 223.   [229] Munzel 1999, 224.

[230] CPR A832-851/B860-79.

[231] In the *Anthropology*, for example, Kant writes: "In the end, since the entire use of the cognitive faculty for its own advancement, even in theoretical cognition, surely requires reason, which gives the rule in accordance with which it alone can be advanced, we can summarize the demand that reason makes on the cognitive faculty in three questions, which are directed to the three cognitive faculties: *What do I want?* (asks understanding), *What does it matter?* (asks the power of judgment), *What comes of it?* (asks reason)" [7: 227]. See also CJ, 5: 294-95.

[232] See G, 4: 433, 4: 439.

have some textual basis in Kant's analysis of the maxim in the third *Critique*, it is mistaken. In the third *Critique*, Kant writes: "The third maxim, namely that of the consistent way of thinking, is the most difficult to achieve, and can only by achieved through the combination of the first two and after frequent observance of them has made them automatic."[233] I do not think that this remark of Kant's supports Deligiorgi's and Munzel's interpretation. Kant asserts in this excerpt that the third maxim, which is the most challenging to follow regularly, can only be implemented after mastering the regular application of the first two maxims. It is possible that learning to consistently abide by the first two maxims is a prerequisite for learning the third. Nevertheless, Kant is not affirming in this passage, as proposed by Deligiorgi and Munzel, that the third maxim solely involves the consistent and regular application of the first two maxims.

Taken together, the three maxims of common human understanding, as O'Neill writes, "are presented as exemplifying the requirements for preserving lawlikeness without assuming a lawgiver."[234] They are supposed to guide our use of reason in thinking and acting so that we can be fully fledged, mature members of the human community. Tying it to the notion of "pluralism" from the published *Anthropology*, these members are pluralists who endorse "the way of thinking in which one is not concerned with oneself as the whole world, but rather regards and conducts oneself as a mere citizen of the world."[235] To regard and conduct oneself as a citizen of the world means to guide one's reason only by the principles that are common to all human beings.

The three maxims of common human understanding are also relevant to Kant's conception of what it means to see the world with a philosophical eye and hence to participate in what he views to be the development of the proper history of philosophy.[236] Unfortunately, his vision of what it means to do philosophy is racially exclusive and limited to the work of the Occidental white thinkers.[237] As Lu-Adler explains, Kant contributed to the eighteenth-century debate about whether philosophy originated in Greece (and hence in the West) or in the "Orient" (Egypt or India) by drawing a contrast between a learned "Cyclops" and a person who sees the world with the systematizing "eye of true philosophy." He characterizes the former as being engaged in a descriptive *historia* of the various empirically known contributions to philosophy, and the latter as developing "a philosophical *Geschichte* in accordance with an idea of reason, so that it includes only those philosophizing attempts that manifest a teleologically oriented history of reason's self-development."[238]

---

[233] CJ, 5: 295. [234] O'Neill 1992, 300. [235] Anth, 7: 130. [236] Reflexionen 15: 396.
[237] Lu-Adler 2023a, 285–328. [238] Lu-Adler 2023a, 290.

Now, Kant presents a racially exclusive account of who is capable of contributing a philosophy in the latter sense.

> For a piece of historical material to qualify as a genuine attempt at philosophizing, Kant stipulates, its author must be someone who was actually capable of forming abstract concepts and principles – in order to set ends and thin systematically – and who lived in a society where one could freely think for oneself and publicize one's thoughts in community of truth seekers.[239]

The conditions include the capacity to orient one's thinking in accordance with the three maxims of common human understanding. But Kant suggests that only the Occidental whites were capable of such a way of thinking and that only them lived in societies that enabled such a way of thinking. Consequently, he claims that philosophy must have originated in Greece and that philosophy proper is limited to the philosophy developed in the West.

3.3 Individual Pluralism, Species Pluralism, and Reason's Future Development

Kant's discourse on the arduous and time-consuming process of cultivating practical reason or learning to adopt the pluralistic standpoint of practical reason is applicable to both the personal growth of an individual throughout their life *and* to the progress of the entire human race across many generations. To some extent, both the human species collectively and each individual must endeavor to attain the maturity of reason. In "What Is Enlightenment?" and in *Anthropology*, Kant talks about the duty of extricating oneself from reason's immaturity (minority)[240] or unfreedom that *every single* individual has: "it is difficult for any single individual to extricate himself from the minority that has become nature to him;" "there are only a few who have succeeded ... in extricating themselves from minority."[241] He also underlines the significance of the task of exiting immaturity of reason by calling it "the most important revolution from within the human being."[242] But Kant is clearly also interested in the rational maturing of the *humankind* as a whole, as he uses phrases such as "universal enlightenment," "humankind's emergence from its self-incurred immaturity," and "an enlightened age."[243]

So it makes sense to ask: what is the connection between these two processes? While Kant does not explicitly delve into this matter, it remains in the

---

[239] Lu-Adler 2023a, 290.

[240] The terms "immaturity" and "minority" as used by different translators to render the same German word "Unmündigkeit" used by Kant.

[241] WIE, 8: 36.   [242] Anth, 7: 229.   [243] WIE, 8: 40.

background when he concedes, toward the conclusion of *Anthropology*, the perplexing and somewhat discouraging nature of humanity's endeavor to educate itself: "The human being must . . . be *educated* to the good; but he who is to educate him is on the other hand a human being who still lies in the crudity of nature and who is now supposed to bring about what he himself needs. Hence the continuous deviation from his vocation with the always-repeated returns to it."[244] In *Lectures on Pedagogy*, Kant similarly observes that humans can only be educated and perfected by other (imperfect) humans, which makes this process challenging, slow, and filled with failed attempts: "The human being can only become human through education. . . . It must be noted that the human being is educated only by human beings, human beings who likewise have been educated. That is also why the lack of discipline and instruction in some people makes them in turn bad educators of their pupils."[245]

This section aims to investigate the relationship between the personal maturation of an individual and the collective maturation of humanity. This inquiry can be subdivided into several more specific questions that I plan to tackle. Firstly, how many individuals within a given community (or globally) must attain maturity for humanity to be considered mature as a whole? Is the maturation of humankind contingent on particular individuals in public positions, such as political leaders, religious figures, or educators? Additionally, how does the maturation of distinct groups of people, such as nations, affect the maturation of the entire human race?

According to Kant, the enlightenment of individuals and that of humanity as a whole are interdependent. That the education of humanity relies on that of individual people may appear obvious since humanity comprises individuals, but that the education of individuals relies on that of humanity is not. As previously noted, Kant contends that the advancement of human capabilities can only transpire within a communal framework. In his *Lectures on Pedagogy*, he asserts that an individual can become progressively more enlightened or mature by obtaining appropriate education from qualified instructors. Kant then divides the education of a human being into three sequential phases: care, discipline, and instruction.[246]

As an infant or toddler, the human being needs the *care* of his parents so that he does not make a harmful use of his powers. (By "harmful" Kant does not mean an act that would be intelligibly evil – toddlers cannot be morally blameworthy – but an act that could harm other people or this child's own development.) The toddler does not take an active role in this stage of his own education, but passively receives help from others. Subsequently, an individual

---

[244] Anth, 7: 325; emphasis original.   [245] Ped, 9: 441–43.   [246] Ped, 9: 441–44.

must be *disciplined* to prevent the influence of their animalistic impulses from obstructing their human development (which is inherently distinct from remaining an animal). Kant characterizes the discipline phase as a negative procedure of restricting one's inclination toward animalistic conduct. It is this process that instills in a child's mind the "principles of reason."[247] Finally, as a young adult or an apprentice, the human being needs to receive *instruction* – the positive part of education – in order to cultivate his rational capacities and moral virtue, and hence to learn to participate not just in the social and technical, but also in the moral life of humanity.[248]

It appears that it is only the third phase of education – instruction – that initiates the progression of acquiring the knowledge necessary to become a pluralist or an enlightened person. Conversely, the first two stages serve the purpose of readying one's mind to be able to accept such instruction and apply it, but do not comprise aspects of the enlightenment process and do not necessitate any active involvement on the student's part. In addition, it is essential for other individuals to be adequately involved in all three phases of education. This implies not only that a child cannot become fully human in isolation, but also that the lack of awareness on the part of others regarding effective education methods will impede a child's prospects of attaining enlightenment and adopting the pluralistic perspective of reason.

Kant believes that since we have not yet discovered the ideal and most effective method of educating children, it is likely that no individual has attained complete enlightenment, although he does not state this explicitly. Nonetheless, the rational advancement of any individual, when returned to the community, will contribute incrementally to the enlightenment of humanity. Subsequently, this will have a positive impact on the intellectual development of individuals in the following generations. Kant expresses this concept of intergenerational education in his *Lectures on Pedagogy*:

> Education is an art, the practice of which must be perfected over the course of many generations. Each generation, provided with the knowledge of the preceding ones, is ever more able to bring about an education which develops all of the human being's natural predispositions proportionally and purposively, thus leading the whole human species toward its vocation.[249]

Kant discusses the stages of the child's education into a fully fledged person in several other places, such as "Universal History," *Anthropology*, and once again

---

[247] Ped, 9: 442.

[248] For a more detailed description of the phases of a child's education, which goes beyond my purposes here, see Munzel 1999: 279–88.

[249] Ped, 9: 446.

later in *Lectures on Pedagogy*. Each time he refers to them as cultivation, civilization, and moralization.[250] Cultivation involves learning how to accomplish a desired end through appropriate means, without yet being able to determine the end for oneself. Civilization, on the other hand, entails acquiring prudence and learning how to behave appropriately in the cultural context in which one lives. Finally, moralization involves the ability to select good ends from a wide range of possible options, "those which are necessarily approved by everyone and which can be the simultaneous ends of everyone."[251]

Each time Kant mentions the three stages of human development, he hints at their close connection with humanity's large-scale rational progress toward fulfilling its vocation. In "Universal History" he talks about cultivation, civilization, and moralization as something that "we," collectively, are involved in.[252] In *Anthropology* he discusses this triad as something the human being is "destined" to achieve as his "vocation" by living "in a society with [other] human beings."[253] Likewise, in *Lectures on Pedagogy* he notes that the development of the individuals through education must "reflect especially on the development of humanity," "try to bring posterity further than they themselves have gone," and must "see to it that humanity becomes not merely skillful but also moral."[254] In this text we also find a more explicit indication that these stages of a person's development are possibly stages of humanity's development, too: "We live in a time of disciplinary training, culture and civilization, but not by any means in a time of moralization."[255] If Kant can use these stages to describe his own era, it suggests that they can apply not only to the phases of an individual's life, but also to humanity's overall progress. Additionally, individuals within a given period have varying levels of development and enlightenment. While it is possible that there are more enlightened people today, or that the educated people of today are more enlightened than their counterparts from a century ago, differences in development and enlightenment still exist within the current generation, as they have in the past.

---

[250] In *Lectures on Pedagogy* [9:449–50], he actually mentions four stages, adding discipline to the beginning of the list. Kant's account of the different stages of education, particularly in *Lectures on Pedagogy*, is inconsistent and not well-presented. This may be due to the fact that these *Lectures* were edited by Kant's former student Friedrich Theodor Rink, who was not always careful with Kant's text.

[251] *Lectures on Pedagogy*, 9: 450. I believe that these three stages correspond, respectively, to the exercise of the technical hypothetical imperative, the pragmatic hypothetical imperative, and the categorical imperative [G 4: 414–7].

[252] IUH, 8: 26.   [253] Anth, 7: 324.   [254] Ped, 9: 449.

[255] Ped, 9: 451. In "What Is Enlightenment?" we find a very similar observation: "If it is now asked whether we at present live in an enlightened age, the answer is: No, but we do live in an age of enlightenment" [8:40].

Kant's frequent assertion that an individual cannot achieve human perfection, destiny, or vocation on their own[256] creates challenges in distinguishing between the process of attaining enlightenment for an individual *versus* for humanity as a whole. At first glance, it may seem obvious that no single individual can fulfill humanity's vocation, given that Kant's focus is on humanity as a collective. However, this oversimplifies Kant's perspective and fails to capture fully the nuances of his ideas. Rather, for Kant the intellectual achievements of one generation are a baseline for the education and development of the generation that is to follow. This is why "the correct concept of the manner of education can only arise if each generation transmits its experience and knowledge to the next, each in turn adding something before handing it over to the next."[257] If a critical number of generations succeeds in this regard, then "education will get better and better and each generation will move one step closer to the perfection of humanity."[258] To ensure that individuals who will live in the future attain enlightenment, it is essential for one generation collectively to take a step toward enlightenment.

But how many individuals in a given community (or in the entire world) must achieve maturity in order for the individuals of the following generation to have the right circumstances for their own enlightenment? And does the maturing of future individuals depend on any particular people? Kant does not provide an answer to the former question, but he provides one to the latter. The maturing of people from the next generation, he says, depends on how enlightened the individuals in public roles – especially teachers, political leaders, and religious leaders – currently are. The primary responsibility of teachers is to develop and implement an appropriate educational plan for schools that aims to improve the human condition: "the design for a plan of education must be made in a *cosmopolitan* manner. ... Accordingly, the set-up for the schools should depend entirely on the judgment of *the most enlightened experts*. ... It is only through the efforts of people ... who take an *interest* in the best world and who are capable of conceiving the idea of a future improved condition, that the gradual approach of human nature to its purpose is possible."[259] Kant publicly expresses great admiration and contentment about one particular educational institution in Prussia – the Philanthropinum Institute in Dessau established by

---

[256] In *Anthropology*, for example, he says: "with all other animals left to themselves, each individual reaches its complete destiny; however with the human being only the species, at best, reaches it" (7:324). In *Universal History* he similarly claims: "*In the human being* (as the only rational creature on earth), *those predispositions whose goal is the use of his reason were to develop completely only in the species, but not in the individual*" [8:18–19; original emphasis]. In *Lectures on Pedagogy*, he claims: "It is also completely impossible for the individual to reach the [human] vocation" [9:445].

[257] Ped, 9: 446.   [258] Ped, 9: 444.   [259] Ped, 9: 448–49; my emphasis.

Johann B. Basedow in 1774 – of which he writes that it is the first institution that "[has] come about according to the perfect plan of education" and is "the greatest phenomenon which has appeared in this century for the improvement of the perfection of humanity."[260] By looking at Kant's description of the teaching methods endorsed by the Dessau Institute and advocated more generally by the Philanthropinismus reform movement, we may perhaps be able to infer how an ideal cosmopolitan plan of education might look like.[261]

The primary goal of this school is to enable its students to become teachers using the true educational method, thereby spreading it throughout the country, and eventually the world. This objective highlights the duty of more enlightened people to enhance the human condition. Indeed, being enlightened means knowing how to improve society by taking on public roles. The Dessau Institute implemented various educational techniques, including de-emphasizing memorization in favor of critical thinking and enjoyable conversation-based learning, combining theoretical instruction with manual labor and physical activities, and teaching foreign languages through conversation. Additionally, the school admitted children from different social classes, religions, and sexes, and encouraged simple attire to minimize class distinctions. These methods align with Kant's emphasis on common human understanding, the development of various skills and talents, and the equal treatment of all individuals. According to Kant's *Lectures on Pedagogy*, teachers have a responsibility to foster not only technical skills but also the ability to think in an enlightened manner (i.e., freely, publicly, and consistently). The best teachers and other public figures try not only to develop the technical and prudential skills of the under their governance, but also their morality, thus "bring[ing] posterity further than they themselves have gone."[262]

In addition to teachers, political leaders and religious authorities also play a key role in the maturing of the generation that follows them. The role of the enlightened political leaders and the state in general is the protection of rightful freedom of its citizens. The state, for example, guards us against civil compulsion and compulsion over conscience. It also ensures the freedom, equality, and independence of each of its citizens. It thereby removes the obstacles to adopting the three maxims of common human understanding and encourages participation in the public domain and law-making. Political leaders and religious authorities also have a significant role to play in the maturation of the following generation, alongside teachers. The state's responsibility, according to Kant, is to safeguard the rightful freedom of its citizens and to protect

---

[260] Anth-Fried, 25: 722–23.
[261] For a comprehensive account of Basedow's progressive ideas on education, see Louden 2020.
[262] Ped, 9: 449–50.

them against civil and religious coercion. Additionally, the state should ensure that every citizen enjoys freedom, equality, and independence,[263] thus paving the way for them to adopt the three maxims of common human understanding and engage in public discourse and lawmaking. Here Kant's idea of a "moral politician" – a leader whose political principles and decisions are compatible with morality[264] – can serve as an illustration of what kind of political leaders would be needed so that the country in question can progress toward enlightenment. Enlightened religious leaders, in turn, are tasked with promoting moral progress and the development of moral virtue in themselves and others, with the aim of transforming our behavior from simply empirically good to intelligibly good – motivated by moral principles.

Another question that arises concerning the relationship between an individual's maturation and the maturation of humanity as a whole is what impact the maturation of specific groups, such as nations, has on the maturation of the entire human species. Kant does not give a clear answer to this question, but its importance for his project is evident from his frequent discussion of the necessity for the educational techniques to be designed "in a cosmopolitan manner" and from the fact that his ideal political state is the cosmopolitan condition ("Universal History"). The term *weltbürglicher* ("cosmopolitan") and its cognates such as *Weltbürger* ("citizen of the world") are technical terms in Kant's philosophy. Crucially, as we have seen earlier, he uses them in the definition of a "pluralist" in *Anthropology*. The widespread, normative use of this term is most evident, however, in the "Theory and Practice" essay where Kant defines the cosmopolitan perspective as "a view to the well-being of the human race as a whole and insofar as it is conceived as progressing toward its well-being in the series of generations of all future times."[265]

Although Kant emphasizes the importance of a cosmopolitan perspective and state of mind, his historical, anthropological, religious, and pedagogical writings primarily focus on Europe, particularly his own country. However, we can speculate on Kant's perspective regarding the impact of different nations' maturation on the entire human species. It is reasonable to assume that, according to Kant, the more enlightened or mature nations would have the obligation to serve as guides and teachers to other nations. In this scenario, the relationship between more and less enlightened nations would be akin to that of a well-trained teacher and the pupils at the Dessau Institute. Additionally, the principles of enlightened governance, education, and general thinking and acting would need to be communicated through international agreements and guidelines for political issues and educational curricula. Kant's reasoning behind this

---

[263] See, for example, TP, 8: 290–96, WOT, 8: 144–45.   [264] TPP, 8: 372.   [265] TP, 8: 277–78.

view is likely that gradual progress for humanity as a whole requires mature nations guiding less mature ones toward enlightenment.[266]

It is also evident from Kant's anthropology lectures, his *Observations* and his three essays on race that Kant's views on human progress and his concept of a *Weltbürger* are heavily racialized. As Lu-Adler has argued, Kant believes that white Westerners are *uniquely* suited to the task of advancing human progress because, due to their privileged location on our planet, they possess exceptional mental capacities.[267] The logical space for this kind of claim is carved out when he suggests that humanity will make moral progress as a species, not as an aggregate of all individuals;[268] due to this, Kant is able to "exclude entire populations – on account of their racialized characteristics, including aptitudes, cognitive (in)abilities, and so on – from playing any agential role in the continued human progress toward the species-bound moral destiny."[269]

Throughout the above-mentioned texts, Kant makes a distinction between four races – white (Europeans), red (Americans), black ("Negroes"), and yellow (Asiatic Indians) – and claims that the racial characteristics caused by climate include not just skin color, but intellectual, moral, and cultural predispositions, too. In the *Menschenkunde* anthropology lectures, for instance, he claims roughly that:

(1) The Americans have no driving force, no affects or passions, and no care for anything. They acquire no culture.
(2) "Negroes" are full of passions. Being sensitive and "afraid of beatings," they can be trained. They are suitable only for a "culture of slaves."
(3) Asiatic Indians or "Hindus" have driving forces and passions, but no ability for abstract thoughts. Accordingly, they can acquire some culture in the arts, but not in the sciences. They have come to a standstill.
(4) The white race contains all the driving forces and talents.[270]

Kant regards "talent" as "natural aptitude, or the capacity to learn, and spirit or genius"[271] and claims that nature has equipped some people in more talent than others. This text as well as Kant's earlier *Observations* heavily implies that, as Lu-Adler puts it, "insofar as nature has generously endowed [the white] race *alone* with all the favorable drives and talents, they also have a *unique calling* to work as the agents propelling the human species toward its final (moral)

---

[266] I am merely reconstructing and filling in Kant's views here, not endorsing them. I do recognize that this picture, unfortunately, has been used to justify colonialism and a multitude of harmful racist attitudes.

[267] Lu-Adler 2023b.

[268] Lu-Adler 2023a, 16–17. The human species, for Kant, constitutes a unified "system," which is not the same as an "aggregate" of individuals (Anth, 7: 320).

[269] Lu-Adler 2023a, 17.   [270] Lu-Adler 2023b, 88. See Me 25: 1187.   [271] Me 25: 1157.

end."[272] The other races are not capable of the kind of culture that constitutes the positive part of Kant's educational plan, and hence of becoming enlightened; their role, rather, is that of a *cautionary tale* for the white race. The Kantian citizen of the world (*Weltbürger*) is thus an Occidental white man uniquely suited to fulfill humankind's duty to perfect itself and realize its vocation.

My hope is that this section of the Element has provided a thorough account of the necessary and collectively sufficient components of adopting a pluralistic standpoint of reason or, simply put, of being a pluralist. As we have seen, these three components are: thinking freely or abiding by the maxim "think for oneself," making public use of reason or abiding by the maxim "think from the standpoint of others," and abiding by the maxim "think consistently." By doing so, I have provided evidence for the claim that Kant's notion of pluralism is not only a political notion, but primarily an ethical one: it pertains both to acting and to structuring one's motivational psychology. Each individual's developing and maintaining a pluralistic standpoint of reason is therefore *necessary* for collectively developing moral principles that govern everyone's actions. I have also shown that Kant is concerned with the process of reason's maturing or enlightenment in both every individual human being and in the human species as a whole.

Conclusion

This Element has been motivated by the fact that while much attention has been given to Kant's historical, anthropological, pedagogical, and religious writings, there is a notable gap in the discussion regarding the inception of humankind's rational progress and the conditions that facilitated this transition from mere animality to primitive rationality.

In Section 1, I have reconstructed Kant's speculative account of the beginning of human rationality and our species' transition from the state of nature to the condition of sociality. I have also discussed his account of the gradual evolution of our species' rational, moral, and sociopolitical abilities. In reconstructing Kant's narrative on the prehistory of reason, one must delve into various conjectural and literal remarks that can be found in "Conjectural Beginning of Human History" and his anthropology lectures. Kant's historical claims, often perceived as speculative or playful, offer significant insights when viewed through the lens of post-facto reflections that aim to make sense of various historical phenomena by imposing a priori conditions on them without making claims as to their empirical accuracy. Kant's narrative in "Conjectural Beginning" uniquely speculates about the transition from animality to rationality, a theme central to Enlightenment

---

[272] Lu-Adler 2023b, 89.

thinkers who engaged in writing conjectural histories. Kant's conjectural history aims to sketch a plausible path for the emergence of humankind's rational capacities, complementing his teleological view of human history without claiming empirical accuracy. In "Conjectural Beginning," Kant provides a speculative account of the first use of reason, which marked the transition from animality to humanity. This pivotal moment involved recognizing alternative possibilities for action beyond instinct, inventing new desires, and making choices independent of natural impulses. This initial exercise of reason led to a growing awareness of human uniqueness and the capacity for free choice, which Kant views as the beginning of rationality and human history. Kant's narrative suggests that the awakening of reason involved several steps, including overcoming natural instincts, manipulating desires, anticipating future challenges, and recognizing human superiority over other animals. These steps reflect a gradual shift toward rational and moral capacities, framing the human being as a unique member of the animal kingdom, capable of acting beyond natural determinations. With the emergence of reason, humans distinguish themselves from other animals by belonging to both the natural and rational realms. This duality allows humans to surpass their animalistic instincts through education, culture, and socialization. Kant emphasizes that human development requires social interaction and education, contrasting with animals that rely solely on instincts for survival. The concept of "unsociable sociability" encapsulates the tension between humans' social inclinations and their individualistic tendencies, driving the progress of human capacities.

In Kant's conjectural story from the "Conjectural Beginning," the initial use of reason had profound effects on human development, leading to both the feeling of discontent and the emergence of evil within human nature. This arose from humans' realization of their ability to control desires, resulting in competitive and self-serving behavior. Kant posits that social interaction was the context in which evil desires and actions first emerged, driven by comparative judgments and competitiveness. The propensity for evil, derived from unsociable sociability, also spurred human advancements such as the arts and sciences. This dual nature of sociality – causing both progress and conflict – highlights the need for just political systems to minimize evil and to promote the good derived from human interaction. Kant's view involves the gradual moralization of society through education, legislation, and religion, with each generation building on the intellectual achievements of the previous one. Enlightened teachers, political leaders, and religious authorities play crucial roles in guiding this progress. The ultimate goal is a cosmopolitan society where individuals act as citizens of the world, governed by universal laws that promote collective well-being. This developmental process underscores the importance of social, political, and educational systems in human moral progress. Kant's vision of a cosmopolitan condition aligns with a moral community where individuals recognize and act on their duties, fostering a progressive, albeit never fully realizable, ethical state. The history of humanity, thus, is a continuous learning process of using reason correctly and overcoming natural inclinations through collective efforts and gradual enlightenment.

Section 2 of this Element focused on situating "Conjectural Beginning" against the backdrop of Enlightenment conjectural histories. I provided a characterization of key features of this genre, drawing on a number of examples. The conjectural history genre emerged in the late seventeenth and early eighteenth centuries as a response to the limitations of traditional historiography, which focused on the actions of elites and major political events. Traditional history was seen as catering to the elite by documenting wars, conquests, and the deeds of prominent leaders, ignoring the lives of ordinary people. This led to a crisis in historiography, highlighting the need for a new genre that addressed the broader audience and included the experiences of various social classes. Conjectural history thus broke with traditional historiography by emphasizing the typical lives of individuals and groups, focusing on diverse events beyond wars and conquests. The typical features of this genre include: focusing on the prehistorical existence of human beings which lies too far in the past for us to have any materials documenting this kind of life; assuming that a specific event in time began human history; postulating specific circumstances of humans' exit from the state of nature and providing an explanation of the reasons for this exit; exhibiting an ambivalent attitude toward progress; abandoning the framework of Genesis and any notion of divine providence; and casting the developmental story of humankind in terms of the original sources that prompt it rather than in a teleological way. Kant's conjectural history adheres to a number of these features, but departs from some of them. In particular, Kant does not follow the trend of abandoning the framework of Genesis and any notion of divine providence. Rather, he draws heavily on the notion of divine Christian providence, and hence recourses to a non-naturalistic explanation of human progress. Second, Kant does not follow other conjectural historians in casting the developmental story of humankind in terms of the original sources that prompt it rather than in a teleological way. Instead, he draws heavily on teleological notions of human progress and perfectionism that are characteristic of his philosophy of history at large.

In Section 3, I have elaborated on Kant's prescriptions for the future of humanity and human reason. As I have shown in Section 1, according to Kant's "Conjectural Beginning" the first humans who started using reason had a tendency toward practical egoism: giving deliberative weight only to one's own happiness. This led to the emergence of an unjust juridical order motivated by individual self-interest and competitiveness. However, the gradual improvement of our juridical order appears to be associated with a psychological disposition that opposes practical egoism: the disposition to pluralism. Kant argues in his essays from the 1780s and in his published *Anthropology* that for a truly just juridical order to exist, its members must be pluralists in his sense of this word. This means assuming and accepting coexistence in a community with others (as world citizens) and regarding oneself as governed by the universal law that regulates the pursuit of different conceptions of happiness. In particular, to be a pluralist means to abide by the maxims "think for oneself" (thinking freely), "think from the standpoint of others" (making public use of one's reason), and "think consistently."

The maturation of reason toward the standpoint of pluralism involves both individual efforts and collective progress, with enlightened education and leadership playing pivotal roles in humanity's journey toward rational and moral maturity. In a number of his works, Kant discusses the development of practical reason, both in individuals and humanity, emphasizing the gradual, challenging process of attaining rational maturity. He highlights the duty of individuals to overcome the immaturity of reason, viewing this as a significant internal revolution. Kant also stresses the collective maturation of humankind, referring to "an enlightened age." Kant acknowledges the difficulty of this process, noting that humans must educate each other despite their imperfections. This mutual education is slow and error-prone, requiring a communal effort across generations. In his *Lectures on Pedagogy*, Kant outlines three phases of education: care, discipline, and instruction. These stages prepare individuals for rational and moral development, ultimately aiming to cultivate enlightened, pluralistic thinkers. Kant argues that humanity's maturation requires a community where education and knowledge are passed down and improved over generations. He emphasizes the role of public figures – teachers, political leaders, and religious authorities – in this process. Enlightened individuals in these roles are crucial for designing and implementing educational plans that foster the development of human potential. Kant also explores the relationship between individual and collective maturation. He posits that the enlightenment of nations impacts the entire human race, with more mature nations guiding others toward enlightenment. This cosmopolitan perspective, aiming for the well-being of humanity, is essential for gradual progress.

References

Allison, Henry (2009). "Teleology and History in Kant: The Critical Foundations of Kant's Philosophy of History." *Kant's "Idea for a Universal History with a Cosmopolitan Aim": A Critical Guide*, ed. Amélie O. Rorty & James Schmidt. Cambridge: Cambridge University Press.

Basedow, Johann B. (1752). *Inusitata et optima honestioris iuverntutis erudiendae methodus*, Magister thesis, University of Kiel.

Basedow, Johann B. (1774). *Das in Dessau errichtete Philanthropinum, eine Schule der Menschenfreundschaf.* Leipzig: Crusius.

Batterman, Robert W. & Collin C. Rice (2014). "Minimal Model Explanations." *Philosophy of Science* 81(3), 349–76.

Beiser, Frederick C. (1987). *The Fate of Reason: German Philosophy from Kant to Fichte*. Cambridge, MA: Harvard University Press.

Berry, Christopher J. (1974). "Adam Smith's Considerations on Language." *Journal of the History of Ideas* 35(1), 130–38.

Booth, W. (2009). "Reason and History: Kant's Other Copernican Revolution." *Kant-Studien* 74(1), 56–71.

Brandt, Reinhard (2007). *Die Bestimmung des Menschen bei Kant*. Hamburg: Meiner.

Brown, Garrett W. (2009). *Grounding Cosmopolitanism: From Kant to the Idea of a Cosmopolitan Constitution*. Edinburgh: Edinburgh University Press.

Caswell, Matthew (2006). "The Value of Humanity and Kant's Conception of Evil." *Journal of the History of Philosophy* 44(4), 635–63.

Cavallar, Georg (2012). "Cosmopolitanisms in Kant's Philosophy." *Ethics and Global Politics* 5(2), 95–118.

Cavallar, Georg (2014). "Sources of Kant's Cosmopolitanism: Basedow, Rousseau, and Cosmopolitan Education." *Studies in Philosophy and Education* 33(4), 369–89.

Chakrabarty, Dipesh (2016). "Humanities in the Anthropocene: The Crisis of an Enduring Kantian Fable." *New Literary History* 47(2–3), 377–97.

Cohen, Alix (2012). "Enabling the Realization of Humanity: The Anthropological Dimension of Education." *Kant and Education: Interpretations and Commentary*, ed. Klas Roth & Chris Supernant. New York: Routledge.

Deligiorgi, Katerina (2002). "Universalizability, Publicity, and Communication: Kant's Conception of Reason." *European Journal of Philosophy* 10(2), 143–59.

Deligiorgi, Katerina (2005). *Kant and the Culture of Enlightenment*. New York: SUNY Press.

Deligiorgi, Katerina (2017). "The Philosopher as Legislator: Kant on History." *The Palgrave Kant Handbook*, ed. M. Altman. London: Palgrave Macmillan.

Evnine, Simon (1993). "Hume, Conjectural History, and the Uniformity of Human Nature." *Journal of the History of Philosophy*, 31(4), 589–606.

Formosa, Paul (2012). "From Discipline to Autonomy: Kant's Theory of Moral Development." *Kant and Education: Interpretations and Commentary*, ed. Klas Roth & Chris Supernant. New York: Routledge.

Forst, Rainer (2017). "Political Liberalism: A Kantian View." *Ethics* 128(1), 123–44.

Frierson, Patrick R. (2013). *What Is the Human Being?* Oxford: Routledge.

Gaus, Gerald (1995). "The Rational, the Reasonable and Justification." *The Journal of Political Philosophy*, 3, 234–58.

Gaus, Gerald. (1999). "Reasonable Pluralism and the Domain of the Political: How the Weaknesses of John Rawls's Political Liberalism can be Overcome by a Justificatory Liberalism." *Inquiry*, 4, 229–58.

Gode, Alexander (1986). "Introduction." *On the Origin of Language: Jean Jacques Rousseau's Essay on the Origin of Languages & Johann Gottfried Herder's Essay On the Origin of Language*, trans. John H. Moran. Chicago: University of Chicago Press.

Grenberg, Jeanine M. (2009). "Social Dimensions of Kant's Conception of Radical Evil." *Kant's Anatomy of Evil*, ed. Sharon Anderson-Gold & Pablo Muchnik. Cambridge: Cambridge University Press.

Guyer, Paul (2009). "The Crooked Timber of Mankind": *Kant's "Idea for a Universal History with a Cosmopolitan Aim" – A Critical Guide*, ed. Amélie O. Rorty & James Schmidt. Cambridge: Cambridge University Press.

Herder, Johann Gottfried (1986). *On the Origin of Language*, trans. John H. Moran. Chicago: University of Chicago Press.

Herder, Johann Gottfried (2015). *On World History: An Anthology*, ed. Hans Adler & Ernest A. Menze. London: Routledge.

Herman, Barbara (2009). "A Habitat for Humanity." *Kant's "Idea for a Universal History with a Cosmopolitan Aim": A Critical Guide*, ed. Amélie O. Rorty & James Schmidt. Cambridge: Cambridge University Press.

Höpfl, Harro M. (1987). "From Savage to Scotsman: Conjectural History in the Scottish Enlightenment." *Journal of British Studies* 17(2), 19–40.

Hume, David (2018). *The Natural History of Religion*. Dallas: Veritatis Splendor Publications.

Kain, Philip J. (1989). "Kant's Political Theory and Philosophy of History." *Clio* 18: 325–45.

Kant, Immanuel (1996a). "An Answer to the Question: What Is Enlightenment?" *Practical Philosophy*, trans. Mary J. Gregor. Cambridge: Cambridge University Press.

Kant, Immanuel (1996b). *What Does It Mean to Orient Oneself in Thinking?* In *Religion and Rational Theology*, trans. Allen W. Wood & George di Giovanni. Cambridge: Cambridge University Press.

Kant, Immanuel (1998). *Religion within the Boundaries of Mere Reason*, trans. Allen W. Wood & George di Giovanni. Cambridge: Cambridge University Press.

Kant, Immanuel (1999a). "On the Common Saying: That May be Correct in Theory, but It Is of No Use in Practice." *Practical Philosophy*, trans. Mary J. Gregor. Cambridge: Cambridge University Press.

Kant, Immanuel (1999b). *The Metaphysics of Morals. Practical Philosophy*, trans. Mary J. Gregor. Cambridge: Cambridge University Press.

Kant, Immanuel (1999c). *Toward Perpetual Peace. Practical Philosophy*, trans. Mary J. Gregor. Cambridge: Cambridge University Press.

Kant, Immanuel (2000). *Critique of the Power of Judgment*. trans. Paul Guyer & Eric Matthews. Cambridge: Cambridge University Press.

Kant, Immanuel (2005). *Notes and Fragments*, trans. Curtis Bowman, Paul Guyer & Frederick Rauscher. Cambridge: Cambridge University Press.

Kant, Immanuel (2006). *Anthropology from a Pragmatic Point of View*, trans. Robert B. Louden. Cambridge: Cambridge University Press.

Kant, Immanuel (2007a). "Conjectural Beginning of Human History." *Anthropology, History, and Education*, trans. Allen. W. Wood. Cambridge: Cambridge University Press.

Kant, Immanuel (2007b). *Idea for a Universal History with a Cosmopolitan Aim. Anthropology, History, and Education*, trans. Allen W. Wood. Cambridge: Cambridge University Press.

Kant, Immanuel (2009). *Critique of Pure Reason*, trans. Paul Guyer & Allen W. Wood. Cambridge: Cambridge University Press.

Kant, Immanuel (2012). *Lectures on Anthropology*, trans. Robert B. Louden & Allen W. Wood. Cambridge: Cambridge University Press.

Kant, Immanuel (2015). *Critique of Practical Reason*, trans. Mary Gregor. Cambridge: Cambridge University Press.

Kleingeld, Pauline (1999). "Kant, History, and the Idea of Moral Development." *History of Philosophy Quarterly* 16(1).

Kleingeld, Pauline (2009). "Kant's Changing Cosmopolitanism." *Kant's "Idea for a Universal History with a Cosmopolitan Aim": A Critical Guide*, ed. Amélie O. Rorty & Kleingeld, Pauline (2012). *Kant and Cosmopolitanism:*

The Philosophical Ideal of World Citizenship. Cambridge: Cambridge University Press.

Kuehn, Manfred (2012). "Kant on Education, Anthropology, and Ethics." *Kant and Education: Interpretations and Commentary*, ed. Klas Roth & Chris Supernant. New York: Routledge.

Lindstedt, D. (2009). "Kant: Progress in Universal History as a Postulate of Practical Reason." *Kant-Studien* 90(2), 129–47.

Louden, Robert B. (2011). *Kant's Human Being: Essays on His Theory of Human Nature.* Oxford: Oxford University Press.

Louden, Robert B. (2016). "Applying Kant's Ethics: The Role of Anthropology." *A Companion to Kant*, ed. Graham Bird. London: Wiley-Blackwell.

Louden, Robert B. (2017). "Becoming Human: Kant's Philosophy of Education and Human Nature." *The Palgrave Kant Handbook*, ed. Matthew Altman. London: Palgrave Macmillan.

Louden, Robert B. (2020). *Johann Bernhard Basedow and the Transformation of Modern Education: Educational Reform in the German Enlightenment.* London: Bloomsbury.

Lu-Adler, Huaping (2023a). *Kant, Race, and Racism: Views from Somewhere.* Oxford: Oxford University Press.

Lu-Adler, Huaping (2023b). "Know Your Place, Know Your Calling: Geography, Race, and Kant's 'World-Citizen.'" *Studia Kantiana* 21(2), 81–96.

Moran, Kate A. (2009). "Can Kant Have an Account of Moral Education?" *Journal of Philosophy of Education* 43(4), 471–84.

Moran, Kate A. (2011). "The Ethical Community as Ground of Moral Action: An Interpretation of the Highest Good." *Rethinking Kant*, vol. 3, ed. Oliver Thorndike. Newcastle upon Tyne: Cambridge Scholars Publishing.

Moran, Kate A. (2012). *Community and Progress in Kant's Moral Philosophy.* Washington, DC: Catholic University of America Press.

Munzel, G. Felicitas (1999). *Kant's Conception of Moral Character: The "Critical" Link of Morality, Anthropology, and Reflective Judgment.* Chicago: University of Chicago Press.

Munzel, G. Felicitas (2003). "Kant on Moral Education, or 'Enlightenment' and the Liberal Arts." *The Review of Metaphysics* 57(1), 43–73.

Neiman, Susan (1994). *The Unity of Reason: Rereading Kant.* New York: Oxford University Press.

O'Neill, Onora (1989). *Constructions of Reason: Explorations of Kant's Practical Philosophy.* New York: Cambridge University Press.

O'Neill, Onora (1992). "Vindicating Reason." In Paul Guyer (ed.), *The Cambridge Companion to Kant.* New York: Cambridge University Press, 280–308.

Palmeri, Frank (2016). *State of Nature, Stages of Society. Enlightenment Conjectural History and Modern Social Discourse*. New York: Columbia University Press.

Parry, Geraint (2006). "Education." *The Cambridge History of Eighteenth-Century Philosophy*, ed. K. Haakonssen. Cambridge: Cambridge University Press.

Patrone, Tatiana (2008). *How Kant's Conception of Reason Implies a Liberal Politics: An Interpretation of the "Doctrine of Right"*. Lewiston: Edwin Mellen Press.

Phillips, Mark S. (2000). *Society and Sentiment Genres of Historical Writing in Britain, 1740–1820*. Princeton: Princeton University Press.

Rawls, John (1993). *Political Liberalism*. New York: Columbia University Press.

Reisert, Joseph R. (2012). "Kant and Rousseau on Moral Education." *Kant and Education: Interpretations and Commentary*, ed. Klas Roth & Chris Supernant. New York: Routledge.

Rousseau, Jean-Jacques (1984). *Discourse on the Origins and Basis of Inequality among Men*, trans. M. Cranston. London: Penguin Books.

Rousseau, Jean-Jacques (1979). *Emile: Or On Education*, trans. A. Bloom. New York: Basic Books.

Rousseau, Jean-Jacques (1986). *On the Origin of Languages*, trans. John H. Moran. Chicago: University of Chicago Press.

Santos Castro, Juan S. (2017). "Hume and Conjectural History." *Journal of Scottish Philosophy*, 15(2), 157–74.

Schneewind, Jerome B. (2009). "Good out of Evil: Kant and the Idea of Unsocial Sociability." *Kant's "Idea for a Universal History with a Cosmopolitan Aim": A Critical Guide*, ed. Amelie O. Rorty & James Schmidt. Cambridge: Cambridge University Press.

Shell, Susan (2015a). "Kant's Lectures on Pedagogy." *Reading Kant's Lectures*, ed. Robert Clewis. Berlin: de Gruyter.

Shell, Susan (2015b). "'More [Than] Human': Kant on Liberal Education and the Public Use of Reason." *In Search of Humanity: Essays in Honor of Cifford Orwin*, ed. Andrea Radasanu. Boston: Lexington Books.

Smalligan Marušić, Jennifer (2017). "Dugald Stewart on Conjectural History and Human Nature." *Journal of Scottish Philosophy*, 15(3), 261–74.

Smith, Adam (1853). *The Theory of Moral Sentiments; or an Essay Towards an Analysis of the Principles by Which Men Naturally Judge Concerning the Conduct and Character, First of Their Neighbours, and Afterwards of Themselves: To Which Is Added, A Dissertation on the Origin of Languages*. London: Bohn's Standard Library.

Stewart, Dugald (1854a). *Dissertation Exhibiting the Progress of Metaphysical, Ethical, and Political Philosophy: The Collected Works of Dugald Stewart*, ed. William Hamilton, 11 vols. Edinburgh: Thomas Constable and Co., vol. 1.

Stewart, Dugald (1854b). *Elements of the Philosophy of the Human Mind: The Collected Works of Dugald Stewart*, vols. 2–4.

Stewart, Dugald (1858). *"Account of the Life and Writings of Adam Smith": The Collected Works of Dugald Stewart*, vol. 10, 5–98.

Stewart, Dugald (2017). *The Collected Works of Dugald Stewart: Biographical Memoirs of Adam Smith, William Robertson, Thomas Reid: To Which Is Prefixed a Memoir of Dugald Stewart – From His Correspondence – By J. Veitch – 1858*. Andesite Press.

Stroud, Scott R. (2005). "Rhetoric and Moral Progress in Kant's Ethical Community." *Philosophy & Rhetoric*, 38(4), 328–54.

Velkley, Richard L (1989). *Freedom and the End of Reason: On the Moral Foundation of Kant's Critical Philosophy*. Chicago: University of Chicago Press.

Weinstock, Daniel (1996). "Natural Law and Public Reason in Kant's Political Philosophy." *Canadian Journal of Philosophy*, 26(3), 389–411.

White Beck, Lewis (1963). "Editor's Introduction." *Kant: On History*, ed. L. White Beck. Indianapolis: The Bobbs-Merrill Company.

Wokler, Robert (1995). "Anthropology and Conjectural History in the Enlightenment." *Inventing Human Science: Eighteenth Century Domains*, ed. C. Fox, R. Porter & R. Wokler. Oakland: University of California Press.

Wood, Allen W. (1991). "Unsociable Sociability: The Anthropological Basis for Kantian Ethics." *Philosophical Topics*, 19(1), 325–51.

Wood, Allen W. (1995). "Kant's Project for Perpetual Peace." *Proceedings of the Eighth International Kant Congress*, vol. 1. Milwaukee: Marquette University Press.

Wood, Allen W. (1999). *Kant's Ethical Thought*. Cambridge: Cambridge University Press.

Wood, Allen W. (2003). "Kant and the Problem of Human Nature." *Essays on Kant's Anthropology*, ed. B. Jacobs & P. Kain. Cambridge: Cambridge University Press.

Wood, Allen. (2007). "Translator's Introduction." In Immanuel Kant, *Anthropology, History, and Education*, ed. Robert Louden and Günter Zöller. Cambridge: Cambridge University Press.

Wood, Allen W. (2009). "Kant's Fourth Proposition: The Unsociable Sociability of Human Nature." *Kant's "Idea for a Universal History with a Cosmopolitan Aim": A Critical Guide*, ed. A. O. Rorty & J. Schmidt. Cambridge: Cambridge University Press.

Yovel, Yirmiyahu (1978). "Kant and the History of Reason." *Philosophy of History and Action. Philosophical Studies Series in Philosophy*, ed. Y. Yovel. Springer: Dordrecht, vol. 11.

Yovel, Yirmiyahu (1989). *Kant and the Philosophy of History*. Princeton: Princeton University Press.

Yovel, Yirmiyahu (2009). "The Highest Good and History in Kant's Thought." *Archiv für Geschichte der Philosophie*, 54(3), 238–83.

Zimmer, Aime Leigh (2022). "Kant's Conjectures: The Genesis of the Feminine." *The Journal of Speculative Philosophy*, 36(2), 183–93.

Cambridge Elements ☰

The Philosophy of Immanuel Kant

Desmond Hogan
Princeton University

Desmond Hogan joined the philosophy department at Princeton in 2004. His interests include Kant, Leibniz and German rationalism, early modern philosophy, and questions about causation and freedom. Recent work includes 'Kant on the Foreknowledge of Contingent Truths,' *Res Philosophica* 91(1) (2014); 'Kant's Theory of Divine and Secondary Causation,' in Brandon Look (ed.) *Leibniz and Kant*, Oxford University Press (2021); 'Kant and the Character of Mathematical Inference,' in Carl Posy and Ofra Rechter (eds.) *Kant's Philosophy of Mathematics Vol. I*, Cambridge University Press (2020).

Howard Williams
University of Cardiff

Howard Williams was appointed Honorary Distinguished Professor at the Department of Politics and International Relations, University of Cardiff in 2014. He is also Emeritus Professor in Political Theory at the Department of International Politics, Aberystwyth University, a member of the Coleg Cymraeg Cenedlaethol (Welsh-language national college) and a Fellow of the Learned Society of Wales. He is the author of *Marx* (1980); *Kant's Political Philosophy* (1983); *Concepts of Ideology* (1988); *Hegel, Heraclitus and Marx's Dialectic* (1989), *International Relations in Political Theory* (1992); *International Relations and the Limits of Political Theory* (1996); *Kant's Critique of Hobbes: Sovereignty and Cosmopolitanism* (2003); *Kant and the End of War* (2012) and is currently editor of the journal Kantian Review. He is writing a book on the Kantian legacy in political philosophy for a new series edited by Paul Guyer.

Allen Wood
Indiana University

Allen Wood is Ward W. and Priscilla B. Woods Professor Emeritus at Stanford University. He was a John S. Guggenheim Fellow at the Free University in Berlin, a National Endowment for the Humanities Fellow at the University of Bonn and Isaiah Berlin Visiting Professor at the University of Oxford. He is on the editorial board of eight philosophy journals, five book series and The Stanford Encyclopedia of Philosophy. Along with Paul Guyer, Professor Wood is co-editor of The Cambridge Edition of the Works of Immanuel Kant and translator of the Critique of Pure Reason. He is the author or editor of a number of other works, mainly on Kant, Hegel and Karl Marx. His most recently published books are *Fichte's Ethical Thought*, Oxford University Press (2016) and *Kant and Religion*, Cambridge University Press (2020). Wood is a member of the American Academy of Arts and Sciences.

About the Series

This Cambridge Elements series provides an extensive overview of Kant's philosophy and its impact upon philosophy and philosophers. Distinguished Kant specialists provide an up-to-date summary of the results of current research in their fields and give their own take on what they believe are the most significant debates influencing research, drawing original conclusions.

Cambridge Elements ≡

The Philosophy of Immanuel Kant

Printed in the United States
by Baker & Taylor Publisher Services